THE
LOST
SCIENCE

THE LOST SCIENCE

SCIENCE

ESOTERIC MATH AND ASTROLOGY TECHNIQUES
FOR THE MARKET TRADER

M. G. BUCHOLTZ, B.Sc., MBA

iUniverse, Inc.
Bloomington

The Lost Science
Esoteric Math and Astrology Techniques for the Market Trader

iUniverse books may be ordered through booksellers or by contacting:

iUniverse
1663 Liberty Drive
Bloomington, IN 47403
www.iuniverse.com
1-800-Authors (1-800-288-4677)

ISBN: 978-1-4759-9302-8 (sc)
ISBN: 978-1-4759-9304-2 (hc)
ISBN: 978-1-4759-9303-5 (ebk)

Library of Congress Control Number: 2013909970

Printed in the United States of America

iUniverse rev. date: 06/17/2013

To my beautiful wife, Jeanne, who continues to inspire me in so many ways and without whose encouragement my published books would not have become reality.

CONTENTS

FIGURES AND TABLES

INTRODUCTION

The investment industry is deeply flawed.

Investment Advisors encourage clients to buy and hold investment products using the argument that investing is a long-term process. Carefully crafted analyst reports and wealth management marketing strategies support this approach. When markets rise, Investment Advisors inform clients that all is well and that their investments will probably continue to rise in value. When markets fall, Investment Advisors quickly remind clients that all is well as over time markets tend to gradually increase in value despite occasional setbacks. Regardless of market ups or downs, the financial industry continues to extract commissions and fees from the client.

I used to be an Investment Advisor. I am well versed in the academic theory and econometric models that underpin the industry. I am well trained in how to sell to clients the notion of buy and hold.

But I no longer subscribe to the decades old theories, to the flawed models, to the nonsense. Several years ago, I turned my back on the financial industry and walked away.

Frustration can be a powerful motivator. I was frustrated with the investment industry and its focus on encouraging people to buy and hold. This frustration motivated me to look deeply into the forces that influence price action on the financial markets. Why do markets rise? Why do markets fall? I came to realize that the financial markets are largely a reflection of the mass psychology of market participants. When traders and investors are feeling positive, they buy. When they are feeling fearful, they sell. These changing emotions are what create changes in price trends.

What then influences these emotions? Many in the investment industry believe that the daily news influences emotion. I take the reverse view. I maintain that the "news" we see, hear and read is created by changing emotions that have already affected the markets.

For example, on days when investor emotion causes a change in price trend, the financial media will craft convincing arguments in an effort to show how a comment by a central banker, a change to an earnings multiple or a shift in an economic indicator explains the change of price trend. These explanations offered up by the media will vary in fervor, depending on how notable the price shift has been.

My research has led me to conclude that the forces of nature that exist in our cosmos are what influence our emotions. My quest to delve into these forces that drive emotion resulted in the publication of my first book, *The Bull, the Bear and the Planets*. In this book I introduced the reader to the basic tenets of how to use financial astrology as a tool to understand when emotion was likely to result in price trend changes.

In my search for a deeper understanding of the forces that drive investor emotion, I have explored market cycles that are based on the planets Saturn, Mars, Jupiter and Uranus. I have studied the Golden Mean, the Golden Sequence, the power of the Moon, planetary transit lines, price square time and the Universal Clock. Collectively, these phenomena are a science. These scientific phenomena correlate to the changing emotion of market participants and thus to price trend changes on the markets. Recognition of these scientific phenomena is due in large part to the brilliant power of scientific minds throughout history including Brahe, Kepler, Galileo, Copernicus and Newton who studied planetary motions and the forces of attraction between celestial bodies. Eminent scientist Stephen Hawking has said that "Newton unified the heavens and the Earth". Einstein, Lemaitre, Gamow and others in the early 20th century added mightily to our insight into the forces of nature with their conclusions that our universe is awash in cosmic radiation originating from the initial hot big bang that created us. Despite these scientific advances, scientists and psychologists still do not completely understand how these forces of nature cause changes to our emotions. The best we can continue to do is to use our understanding of celestial events in combination with mathematics to anticipate market trend changes. Unfortunately, in our fast paced society, there is a growing tendency for market participants to cast aside concepts which cannot be quickly explained in 140 Twitter characters.

Fear, therefore, has also powerfully motivated me. The *Lost Science* is designed to acquaint market traders and investors with these scientific phenomena that are increasingly in danger of becoming lost. Each day we are inundated with new investment ideas from analysts, business TV hosts and even from colorful television characters who scream "booh-yah" and "buy, buy, buy" as they invoke crazy sound effects on their studio sets. As these distractions mount, I fear that we risk losing touch with the awareness that forces of nature influence the financial markets.

By understanding and carefully applying phenomena such as square root mathematics, lunar cycles, planetary transit lines, the mathematics of the Golden Mean and more, we can maintain a respect for them and thereby make more timely investment and trading decisions.

In Chapter One, you will read about the Golden Mean and a unique method of expressing market cycles in terms of Moons. Chapter Two will show you how support and resistance price levels align to planetary transit lines. Chapter Three delves into square root mathematics, the Square of Nine and Gann lines. Chapter Four questions the long standing notion of charting price data starting at January 1 of a given year. In Chapter Five, you will learn about the charting patterns used by the late Harold Gartley during his successful Wall Street career. After reading Chapter Six, you will have a new respect for the power of the Moon. Chapter Seven will show you how the movements of planets over time can align to market cycles. Lastly, in Chapter Eight, you will see how W.D. Gann and Louise McWhirter in the 1920s and 1930s used astrological techniques to predict the key dates in each month when markets would be most likely to experience changes in price trend.

After applying the concepts presented in this book, I sincerely hope you will come to view the financial markets in a more dynamic way. I hope you will take time to deeply reflect on the power of our cosmos. I hope you will even seek to further your knowledge of the phenomena you will read about in this book.

It is time to break free of the buy and hold mentality.

Your journey to become acquainted with the Lost Science begins now.

CHAPTER ONE

The house which King Solomon built for the Lord was sixty cubits long, twenty cubits wide and thirty cubits high. The vestibule in front of the nave was twenty cubits long equal to the width of the house and ten cubits deep in front of the house. 1 Kings 6: 2-3, *The Bible*

The Golden Mean

The Dark Ages

For thousands of years, mankind has been fascinated with the mathematical relationships between numbers. Some of these numerical relationships are so intriguing that over time they have come to be regarded as sacred and treasured. But the treasured documents underpinning these mathematical relationships nearly came to be lost in 410 AD when the Roman Empire collapsed after Alaric and his Goths sacked the city of Rome. The legions of soldiers and elegant architecture of Rome gave way to a tide of barbarians and the Dark Ages set in across the lands. Pursuit of knowledge gave way to pursuit of hostility.

Enlightenment

In 600 AD, a society known as the Arabs left Mecca (located in modern day Saudi Arabia) under inspiration from their leader Mohammed. They ransacked places like Damascus, Jerusalem and Alexandria taking with them not only the usual spoils of war but also knowledge in the form of old Greek manuscripts. To this ancient Greek knowledge, they added the arithmetic and astrological knowledge of the ancient Hindus. By 650 AD, Baghdad had grown to become the cultural epi-center of the East.

1

Meanwhile, in the West, the remnants of the former Roman Empire came to be reconfigured into the Kingdom of Francia which encompassed much of modern day Europe. In 768 AD, an energetic, charismatic leader by the name of Charlemagne was crowned Emperor of Francia and immediately revived the pursuit of learning and knowledge. The Dark Ages that had spread across the former Roman Empire were finally over.

The pursuit of knowledge was given further impetus in 1000 AD with the election of Pope Sylvester II who revived interest in the seven liberal arts (grammar, rhetoric, logic, arithmetic, geometry, music and astronomy) across the Christian World. Between 1000 AD and 1100 AD, East met West as Arabic knowledge melded with Christian desire for learning. Ancient Greek mathematical works like *Euclid's Elements* were translated into Latin along with various other ancient works.

Filius Bonacci and phi

In 1170 AD a son was born in Pisa to an Italian merchant and his wife. The merchant's name was Bonacci and the son was named Leonardo. In the language of the day, 'filius' meant 'son of' and before long young Leonardo became known as Filius Bonacci which became shortened to Fibonacci. Leonardo spent much of his youth in Barbary (modern day Spain) where his father operated the Customs House. Leonardo had the great fortune to gain exposure to much of the old Greek and Arabic mathematical knowledge while spending time in Barbary. In 1202, he published the now famous *Liber Abaci* in which he demonstrated how to solve quadratic equations. Leonardo also became proficient in Pythagorean mathematics and Euclidean geometry. One of the geometrical constructs Leonardo focused on was the Golden Mean.

Figure 1-1 shows a rectangle divided into two parts (part 'a' and part 'b').

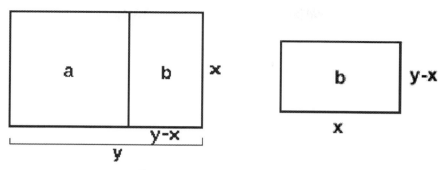

Figure 1-1 The Golden Mean

There is only one point where this rectangle can be divided into parts 'a' and 'b' such that the following ratio holds:

y /x = x/(y-x)

To solve this equation one of the variables must be eliminated. So, let x=1. The expression above then becomes:

$$y = 1 / (y - 1)$$

Multiplying both halves of this expression by (y-1) yields the quadratic expression:

$$y^2 - y - 1 = 0$$

The one and only viable solution to this quadratic expression is:

$$(1 + \sqrt{5}) / 2$$

Solving this expression yields 1.618, the *Golden Mean*, also called *phi* and denoted by the symbol Φ.

Phi (Φ) is elegant and mystical.

Of the mathematical relations known to Greek and Arabic mathematicians, phi (Φ) was probably the most powerful. Hence, its esteemed status as a sacred mathematical term.

The number 1.618 (phi or Φ) derives its name from 5th century Greek sculptor Phidas who used it in creating the proportions of the 9 meter high Athena Parthenos statue and the 13 meter high statue of Zeus in BC 430. But, as English explorer Howard Vyse noted in 1837, the ancient Egyptians also understood the concept of phi (Φ) long before the Greeks. Vyse observed that the angle of inclination of the pyramid of Cheops is 51 degrees, 51 minutes. Vyse calculated the trigonometric relation 'tangent' of 51 degrees, 51 minutes and arrived at 1.273 which he noted to be the square root of phi (Φ).

When contemplating phi (Φ), it is interesting to study the inverse ratios of it. Figure 1-2 presents some of these ratios. Notice how these numbers increase by the multiple of 1.618. That is, 0.146 x 1.618 = 0.236 and so on.

Ratios of ϕ		Inverse Ratios of ϕ	
ϕ	1.618	$\dfrac{1}{\phi}$	.618
ϕ^2	2.618	$\dfrac{1}{\phi^2}$	.382
ϕ^3	4.236	$\dfrac{1}{\phi^3}$	.236
ϕ^4	6.854	$\dfrac{1}{\phi^4}$	.146

Figure 1-2 Inverse Ratios of phi (Φ)

Ratios of $\sqrt{\phi}$		Inverse Ratios of $\sqrt{\phi}$	
$\sqrt{\phi}$	1.272	$\dfrac{1}{\sqrt{\phi}}$	.786
$\sqrt{\phi^2}$	1.618	$\dfrac{1}{\sqrt{\phi^2}}$	.618
$\sqrt{\phi^3}$	2.058	$\dfrac{1}{\sqrt{\phi^3}}$	.486
$\sqrt{\phi^4}$	2.618	$\dfrac{1}{\sqrt{\phi^4}}$	.382
$\sqrt{\phi^5}$	3.330	$\dfrac{1}{\sqrt{\phi^5}}$	.300
$\sqrt{\phi^6}$	4.236	$\dfrac{1}{\sqrt{\phi^6}}$	.236

Figure 1-3 Inverse Ratios of $\sqrt{\Phi}$

It is likewise interesting to study the inverse of the square roots of phi as shown in Figure 1-3. Notice that these numbers increase by a multiple of 1.272 which is the square root of phi (Φ). That is, 0.236 x 1.272 = 0.300 and so on.

Using the Inverse Ratios as part of a Trading Strategy

Stock prices, commodity prices and index values move in distinct waves. In a rising market, buyers—driven by emotion—bid prices higher until the short run marginal benefit of owning the investment is outweighed by the short run marginal economic risk of buying it. Price action then will recede for a period of time before staging another advance. In a falling market, shareholders sell until price reaches a point where emotion changes and more buyers than sellers are attracted to the investment. Then price action will advance for a period of time as buyers again weigh benefits versus risks.

When studying waves of price action on stocks and commodities, the Golden Mean and its various ratios are often evident. Consider just how often the Golden Mean can be found in science and nature. It then stands to reason that the Golden Mean can play a role in the emotional behaviour of buyers and sellers across financial markets. For example, in the human body we have one nose, two eyes and three segments to our limbs. Our arm consists of the segment from the shoulder to the elbow, the segment from the elbow to the wrist and the segment from the wrist to the finger tips. Our leg consists of the segment from the hip to the knee, the segment from the knee to the ankle and the segment from the ankle to the tips of our toes. One, two and three are all related to the Golden Mean. As a practical exercise, measure the distance from your wrist to your fingertips. Divide this measurement by the distance from your elbow to your wrist. Examine the resulting number and you will find a ratio of the Golden Mean at work.

Figure 1-4 illustrates weekly price action of the TSX Composite Index (the Index that tracks the performance of the Toronto Stock Exchange) from the March 2009 low to the March 2011 peak and then to the subsequent October 2011 low. The increase from the 2009 low to the 2011 peak is a move of 5471 points on a close to close basis. The decline into the October 2011 lows on a close to close basis was 2086 points. This decline expressed as a ratio of the increase equates to 0.381. This figure closely approximates the figure 0.382 which is the inverse ratio of the root of phi (Φ) raised to the 4th power. As this October 2011 sell-off was taking place, many traders and investors who were unaware of esoteric mathematical phenomena were shifting into panic mode. In hindsight we now see that this move down was nothing more than an orderly market retracement in harmony with science and nature.

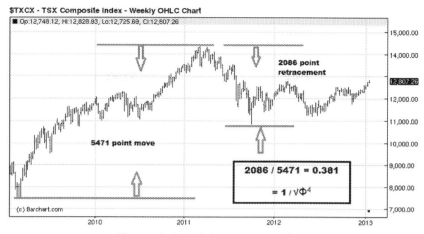

Figure 1-4 TSX Composite Index

For traders who regularly use trading platforms that come complete with built-in suites of technical indicators, the above example will immediately be recognized as what is referred to colloquially as a 38% Fibonacci retracement. By the end of this Chapter, I trust you will have a heightened understanding for the mathematics behind the value of phi (Φ) and a new respect for how phi (Φ) can operate in elegant harmony with the markets.

If you do not regularly use such retracements as part of your trading regimen, I encourage you to study price charts across many different time frames. Calculate the price move between two points in time and then express any subsequent retracement move as a ratio and you will very often see phi (Φ) in some form or another making its presence felt. You may see a ratio involving the inverse of phi (Φ) raised to a power 'n'. You may also see a ratio involving the inverse root of phi (Φ) raised to a power 'n'.

Figure 1-5 illustrates some examples of what you may come across in your chart studies. In Chapter 5, I will dig deeper into phi (Φ) with some very special chart patterns.

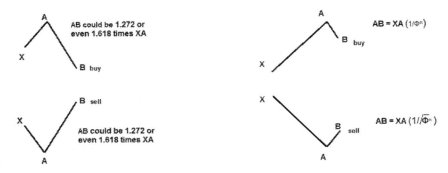

Figure 1-5 Chart Patterns with ratios of phi (Φ)

The Golden Sequence

Demonstrating the construct of phi (Φ) to post-Dark-Ages society was significant in itself. But, Fibonacci brought the concept of phi (Φ) to the forefront of 13th century mathematical thinking when he demonstrated its sequential properties. By raising phi (Φ) to a sequence of incrementally higher exponential powers, he demonstrated the construct of what is called the *Golden Sequence* which has unique additive characteristics.

Fibonacci expressed the uniqueness of the Golden Sequence in layman's terms with his story of two rabbits. In his story, a farmer starts with a breeding pair of rabbits (one male and one female) in his field. After month 2, the female rabbit produces a pair of offspring (one male and one female). She produces another pair of offspring each and every month that follows. A given pair of offspring can begin producing pairs of offspring after they are two months old. After the first month, the farmer has only one pair of rabbits. After the second month he will have two pairs. After the third month he will have three pairs of rabbits as the original female gives birth. After the fourth month, the original female produces yet another pair and the female born two months ago produces a pair, giving the farmer five pairs of rabbits. As an interesting exercise, work this rabbit example further to see for yourself the beauty and harmony of the Golden Sequence.

This sequence was dubbed the *Fibonacci sequence* by French mathematician Eduard Lucas in the late 1800s.

Table 1-1 shows the first 27 terms of the sequence which goes 1, 1, 2, 3, 5, 8, 13 . . . .

Note that a given term of the sequence is the sum of the two preceding numbers in the sequence. Rounded to the nearest integer, the expression $F(n) = (1.618)^n/\sqrt{5}$ will also produce the various Fibonacci sequence numbers.

Column three of Table 1-1 shows how the result of dividing a given term of the sequence by the prior term will converge to 1.618 which is phi (Φ).

As a further interesting exercise, column four of the Table takes the individual digits of a term of the sequence and sums them. The results run the gamut from 1 to 9. Ancient societies regarded the number nine to be sacred and representative of three trinities and also of perfection, balance and order. Note also that the sum of any 10 consecutive numbers is divisible by 11. Every 4th term of the sequence is divisible by 3. Every 5th term is divisible by 5. Every 6th term is divisible by 8. These divisors themselves are the corresponding terms of the sequence. For any four consecutive numbers of the sequence, ABC and D, the relation $C^2-B^2 = A \times D$ holds.

Harmonic and beautiful indeed.

Term of Sequence (n)	F(n) = (1.618)^n/$\sqrt{5}$	(Fn)/(Fn-1)	K (F n)
1	1	1	1
2	1	1	1
3	2	2	2
4	3	1.5	3
5	5	1.66	5
6	8	1.6	8
7	13	1.625	4
8	21	1.615	3
9	34	1.619	7
10	55	1.617	1
11	89	1.618	8
12	144	1.618	9
13	233	1.618	8
14	377	1.618	8
15	610	1.618	7
16	987	1.618	6
17	1597	1.618	4
18	2584	1.618	1
19	4181	1.618	5
20	6765	1.618	6
21	10946	1.618	2
22	17711	1.618	8
23	28657	1.618	1
24	46368	1.618	9
25	75025	1.618	1
26	121393	1.618	1
27	196418	1.618	2

Table 1-1 Golden Sequence

The Spiral Calendar™

While researching this book, I came across many unique applications of the Golden Sequence to trading, some of which tie directly to astrology. Perhaps the most elegant such treatment is called the *Spiral Calendar* which was developed and trademarked by former exchange floor trader Christopher Carolan. Carolan's resulting book entitled the *Spiral Calendar* is a riveting read as he demonstrates the use of Moons as an effective way of measuring time across the history of the financial markets. I highly recommend obtaining a copy of his book.

To demonstrate the power of the Spiral Calendar, Table 1-2 lists the first 27 terms of the Golden Sequence. The column third from left shows the square root of each of the various Golden Sequence terms. The Spiral Calendar methodology assigns a value of Moons to these square root terms. That is, one Moon cycle is taken as 29.5 days. Multiplying 29.5 by the square root term yields the values in the column 4th from left. (ie the root of the third term of the Golden Sequence is 1.41. 29.5 times 1.41 gives 41.8 days).

Term of Sequence (n)	$F(n) = (1.618)^n/\sqrt{5}$	$\sqrt{F(n)}$	Days	Years
1	1	1	29.5	0.1
2	1	1	29.5	0.1
3	2	1.41	41.8	0.1
4	3	1.73	51.1	0.1
5	5	2.24	66.0	.2
6	8	2.83	83.5	.2
7	13	3.61	106.5	.3
8	21	4.58	135.3	.4
9	34	5.83	172.2	.5
10	55	7.42	219.0	.6
11	89	9.43	278.6	.8
12	144	12.00	354.4	1
13	233	15.26	450.8	1.2
14	377	19.42	573.4	1.6
15	610	24.70	729.4	2.0
16	987	31.42	927.7	2.5
17	1597	39.96	1180.1	3.2
18	2584	50.83	1501.1	4.1
19	4181	64.66	1909.5	5.2
20	6765	82.25	2428.9	6.6
21	10946	104.62	3089.6	8.5
22	17711	133.08	3930.0	10.8
23	28657	169.28	4999.1	13.7
24	46368	215.33	6358.9	17.4
25	75025	273.91	8088.6	22.1
26	121393	348.41	10288.9	28.2
27	196418	443.19	13097.7	35.8

Table 1-2 Square Roots of Golden Sequence Terms

Trading the Markets using the Spiral Calendar ™ Technique

Picking up on the example of the TSX Composite Index illustrated in Figure 1-4, the calendar day count from the March 2009 low to the March 2011 high totals 728 days. Looking at the 15th term of the Golden Sequence in Table 1-2, one can see it is 610. The square root of 610 is 24.7 Moons or 729.4 days according to Carolan's Spiral Calendar approach. Clearly then, the TSX Composite Index was behaving in harmony with science and nature as it reached its peak in March 2011. The time from the March 2011 peak to the October 2011 low totalled 209 calendar days. A look again at Table 1-2 shows the 10th term of the Golden Sequence to be 55. The square root of 55 is 7.42 Moons or 219 days according to Carolan's Spiral Calendar approach. Once again, the TSX Composite Index was behaving in very close harmony with science and nature as it declined into its October 2011 low.

As you review price charts of stocks and commodities that you regularly trade, look for significant highs and lows. Look for price advancements and retracements. Use the power of phi (Φ) and its various ratios to anticipate future trend turning points. Consider also becoming more familiar with Carolan's Spiral Calendar approach.

CHAPTER TWO

Astrology is a language. If you understand this language, the sky speaks to you.

Dane Rudhyar-astrologer

The Power of Planetary Transits

There are many ways to apply astrology to the trading of the financial markets. Some traders look for significant price points to align with Full Moons or New Moons. Some look for various aspects between planets to likewise align to significant swings in price. In my recent book *The Bull, the Bear and the Planets*, I offer many examples to show the reader the power of astrology.

But, there is one astrological technique that continues to amaze me with its awesome power. Each time I use this approach, I find myself pausing to reflect on the harmony of the markets with science and nature. What I refer to is the plotting of planetary transit lines on top of price charts for stocks and commodities.

The Wheel of 24

In order to overlay transit lines on price charts, one must become comfortable with the notion of expressing degrees of planetary motion (as determined from the zodiac wheel) in terms of price. At first blush, the visceral instinct is to say that degrees of motion are in no way related to price. But, thanks to the works of W.D. Gann there is a way to convert degrees of motion to price and it is called the *Wheel of 24*.

Figure 2-1 illustrates the Wheel of 24. The image for this Figure has been gleaned from a 1980s publication by trader and author

Jeanne Long. Long took the basic concept of the Wheel of 24 as posited by Gann and trademarked it as her *Universal Clock*.

The Wheel of 24 (Universal Clock) is divided into an inner ring and an outer ring. The inner ring displays the numbers 1 through 360, with these numbers advancing by an increment of 1 in a counter-clockwise direction. These numbers comprise 15 revolutions of the twenty four wheel segments. The figure of 360 is also a very close approximation to the 365 days of our calendar year. The outer ring presents price data. From the 90 degree position where the number 1 appears, move right until you hit the outer ring. This is where the first entry of the price data will appear. Generally, the price data entries will be structured so that from lowest to highest the outer ring data takes into account the entire price range of the stock or commodity over the past 365 days. The price data advances by a suitably chosen increment so that in about 8 or so revolutions of the Wheel of 24, the desired price range can be expressed.

You may find yourself pausing at this point to deeply ponder the Wheel of 24 as it is a unique concept for many traders and investors that can stretch the mind and the sensibilities.

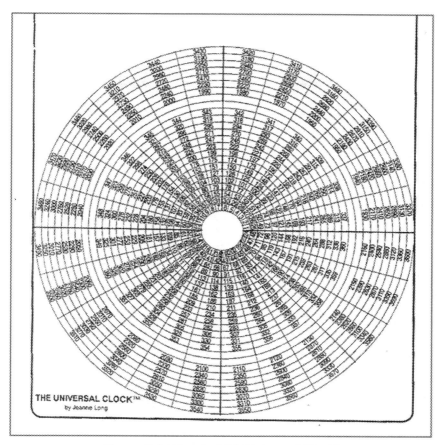

Figure 2-1 Wheel of 24 (Universal Clock)

With price data placed on the Wheel, the next step is to use the Wheel to help create planetary transit lines. In Gann's day, data would have to be entered on a blank copy of a Wheel sketched on a piece of paper—a time consuming exercise indeed. Thankfully technology now makes working with this Wheel a bit easier. There are software programs available that provide you with nice neat circular printouts of this Wheel. However, these software programs retail for up to $3000. I have avoided buying these expensive programs, opting instead for the simplicity of a Microsoft Excel spreadsheet.

Figure 2-2 presents a printed image of a typical Excel spreadsheet that I use to mimic the Wheel of 24. The upper part of the spreadsheet corresponds to the inner part of the Wheel and contains the numbers 1 through 360. The lower part of the spreadsheet corresponds to the outer part of the Wheel and contains the price data. The particular spreadsheet shown in Figure 2-2 is one that I used for a planetary plotting exercise pertaining to the S&P TSX Composite Index (the Index that tracks the performance of the Toronto Stock Exchange). The price data was chosen to cover the high to low range of prices for the time period I was interested in, which was calendar year 2012. Note that I opted to increase the price figures by an increment of 10 points from cell to cell on the spreadsheet. Depending on the stock or commodity under consideration, you can select a price increment to suit yourself. The smaller the increment, the more data you will generate in the outer Wheel and the more work you will make for yourself. Picking too large of an increment will hinder the accuracy of your work, so it becomes a trade-off.

At this point you may want to open your Excel program (or equivalent spreadsheet program if you are not a Microsoft user) and try creating a spreadsheet to mimic the one in Figure 2-2.

The next task is to acquire planetary position data for the planet in question whose transit lines you wish to plot. For this, you should use the data from an Ephemeris. I use the *New American Ephemeris for the 21st Century* which is readily available at most bookstores. You may also be able to find planetary data on-line at by searching for astrological websites. Appendix B provides a short refresher on how to obtain planetary positional data from an Ephemeris.

Saturn Transit Lines

When working with planetary transit lines, I focus on the larger planets, namely Saturn, Jupiter and Uranus. In financial astrology these planets are deemed to have powerful effects on the mass psychology that influences market price action.

Let's consider the case of Saturn for calendar year 2012. Saturn is a slower moving planet, so it should only take a single data point from the middle of each month in order to acquire sufficient data to complete the transit plotting exercise. The positional data as provided in an Ephemeris table will describe the planet as being between 0 and 30 degrees of a given zodiac sign. Recall that 12 zodiac signs of 30 degrees each collectively make up the 360 degrees of the zodiac. Therefore the number gleaned from the Ephemeris must be converted to its 360 degree equivalent. Table 2-1 provides an easy-to-use conversion table that you may wish to refer to. Table 2-2 presents the Saturn data points from the middle of each month during 2012 along with their converted equivalents.

Zodiac Sign	From Degrees to Degrees
Aries	0 degrees to 30 degrees
Taurus	30 degrees to 60 degrees
Gemini	60 degrees to 90 degrees
Cancer	90 degrees to 120 degrees
Leo	120 degrees to 150 degrees
Virgo	150 degrees to 180 degrees
Libra	180 degrees to 210 degrees
Scorpio	210 degrees to 240 degrees
Sagittarius	240 degrees to 270 degrees
Capricorn	270 degrees to 300 degrees
Aquarius	300 degrees to 330 degrees
Pisces	330 degrees to 360 degrees

Table 2-1 Conversion of Zodiac Positions to
360 Degree Equivalents

1	2	3	4	5	6	7	8	9	10	11	12	13	14	15	16	17	18	19	20	21	22	23	24
1	2	3	4	5	6	7	8	9	10	11	12	13	14	15	16	17	18	19	20	21	22	23	24
25	26	27	28	29	30	31	32	33	34	35	36	37	38	39	40	41	42	43	44	45	46	47	48
49	50	51	52	53	54	55	56	57	58	59	60	61	62	63	64	65	66	67	68	69	70	71	72
73	74	75	76	77	78	79	80	81	82	83	84	85	86	87	88	89	90	91	92	93	94	95	96
97	98	99	100	101	102	103	104	105	106	107	108	109	110	111	112	113	114	115	116	117	118	119	120
121	122	123	124	125	126	127	128	129	130	131	132	133	134	135	136	137	138	139	140	141	142	143	144
145	146	147	148	149	150	151	152	153	154	155	156	157	158	159	160	161	162	163	164	165	166	167	168
169	170	171	172	173	174	175	176	177	178	179	180	181	182	183	184	185	186	187	188	189	190	191	192
193	194	195	196	197	198	199	200	201	202	203	204	205	206	207	208	209	210	211	212	213	214	215	216
217	218	219	220	221	222	223	224	225	226	227	228	229	230	231	232	233	234	235	236	237	238	239	240
241	242	243	244	245	246	247	248	249	250	251	252	253	254	255	256	257	258	259	260	261	262	263	264
265	266	267	268	269	270	271	272	273	274	275	276	277	278	279	280	281	282	283	284	285	286	287	288
289	290	291	292	293	294	295	296	297	298	299	300	301	302	303	304	305	306	307	308	309	310	311	312
313	314	315	316	317	318	319	320	321	322	323	324	325	326	327	328	329	330	331	332	333	334	335	336
337	338	339	340	341	342	343	344	345	346	347	348	349	350	351	352	353	354	355	356	357	358	359	360

11000	11010	11020	11030	11040	11050	11060	11070	11080	11090	11100	11110	11120	11130	11140	11150	11160	11170	11180	11190	11200	11210	11220	11230
11240	11250	11260	11270	11280	11290	11300	11310	11320	11330	11340	11350	11360	11370	11380	11390	11400	11410	11420	11430	11440	11450	11460	11470
11480	11490	11500	11510	11520	11530	11540	11550	11560	11570	11580	11590	11600	11610	11620	11630	11640	11650	11660	11670	11680	11690	11700	11710
11720	11730	11740	11750	11760	11770	11780	11790	11800	11810	11820	11830	11840	11850	11860	11870	11880	11890	11900	11910	11920	11930	11940	11950
11960	11970	11980	11990	12000	12010	12020	12030	12040	12050	12060	12070	12080	12090	12100	12110	12120	12130	12140	12150	12160	12170	12180	12190
12200	12210	12220	12230	12240	12250	12260	12270	12280	12290	12300	12310	12320	12330	12340	12350	12360	12370	12380	12390	12400	12410	12420	12430
12440	12450	12460	12470	12480	12490	12500	12510	12520	12530	12540	12550	12560	12570	12580	12590	12600	12610	12620	12630	12640	12650	12660	12670
12680	12690	12700	12710	12720	12730	12740	12750	12760	12770	12780	12790	12800	12810	12820	12830	12840	12850	12860	12870	12880	12890	12900	12910
12920	12930	12940	12950	12960	12970	12980	12990	13000	13010	13020	13030	13040	13050	13060	13070	13080	13090	13100	13110	13120	13130	13140	13150
13160	13170	13180	13190	13200	13210	13220	13230	13240	13250	13260	13270	13280	13290	13300	13310	13320	13330	13340	13350	13360	13370	13380	13390
13400	13410	13420	13430	13440	13450	13460	13470	13480	13490	13500	13510	13520	13530	13540	13550	13560	13570	13580	13590	13600	13610	13620	13630
13640	13650	13660	13670	13680	13690	13700	13710	13720	13730	13740	13750	13760	13770	13780	13790	13800	13810	13820	13830	13840	13850	13860	13870
13880	13890	13900	13910	13920	13930	13940	13950	13960	13970	13980	13990	14000	14010	14020	14030	14040	14050	14060	14070	14080	14090	14100	14110
14120	14130	14140	14150	14160	14170	14180	14190	14200	14210	14220	14230	14240	14250	14260	14270	14280	14290	14300	14310	14320	14330	14340	14350
14360	14370	14380	14390	14400	14410	14420	14430	14440	14450	14460	14470	14480	14490	14500	14510	14520	14530	14540	14550	14560	14570	14580	14590

Figure 2-2 Excel Spreadsheet to Approximate the
Wheel of 24

Month	Saturn Position at mid-Month as taken from the Ephemeris	360 degree Equivalent
January	29 degrees Libra	209 degrees
February	29 degrees Libra	209 degrees
March	28 degrees Libra	208 degrees
April	26 degrees Libra	206 degrees
May	24 degrees Libra	204 degrees
June	22 degrees Libra	202 degrees
July	23 degrees Libra	203 degrees
August	25 degrees Libra	205 degrees
September	27 degrees Libra	207 degrees
October	1 degree Scorpio	211 degrees
November	4 degrees Scorpio	214 degrees
December	8 degrees Scorpio	218 degrees

Table 2-2 Saturn positional data for 2012

Now, this is where I find it gets particularly interesting. The next step is to pick off price data from the spreadsheet you are using to mimic the Wheel of 24 for each of the degree positions determined in Table 2-2. To do this, simply locate each of the degree readings in the upper part of the spreadsheet and then pick off several of the price readings from the same column in the lower part of the spreadsheet. You will then be plotting these price readings on a chart of the S&P TSX Composite Index for 2012. By joining the data points, you will then be able to sketch in the Saturn transit lines.

To assist you, Table 2-3 lists the price data that one would seek to plot on a chart of the TSX Index. Examine this data carefully and make certain you understand how it was derived from the spreadsheet.

Month	360 degree Equivalent	Data Point	Data Point	Data Point	Data Point	Data Point	Data Point	Data Point	Data Point
January	209 degrees	11160	11400	11640	11880	12120	12360	12600	12840
February	209 degrees	11160	11400	11640	11880	12120	12360	12600	12840
March	208 degrees	11150	11390	11630	11870	12110	12350	12590	12830
April	206 degrees	11130	11370	11610	11850	12090	12330	12570	12810
May	204 degrees	11110	11350	11590	11830	12070	12310	12550	12790
June	202 degrees	11090	11330	11570	11810	12050	12290	12530	12770
July	203 degrees	11100	11340	11580	11820	12060	12300	12540	12780
August	205 degrees	11120	11360	11600	11840	12080	12320	12560	12800
September	207 degrees	11140	11380	11620	11860	12100	12340	12580	12820
October	211 degrees	11180	11420	11660	11900	12140	12380	12620	12860
November	214 degrees	11210	11450	11690	11930	12170	12410	12650	12890
December	218 degrees	11250	11490	11730	11870	12210	12450	12690	12930

Table 2-3 Saturn data as obtained from the S&P TSX
Index spreadsheet

For each month in Table 2-3, plot the eight data points on a weekly chart of the S&P TSX Composite Index. I have completed this exercise using a chart generated from www.barchart.com. The result is shown in Figure 2-3. What this chart with Saturn transit lines reveals is nothing short of awe-inspiring. The Saturn transit lines actually correspond to areas of support and resistance encountered during the 2012 calendar year for the S&P TSX Composite Index.

As an interesting exercise, you can next calculate the various data points for the 2013 calendar year. With these data points in hand, you will have a roadmap of what to expect for the S&P TSX Composite Index in 2013. Such a roadmap is a valuable predictive tool that the vast majority of market participants who are unaware of astrological phenomena do not have.

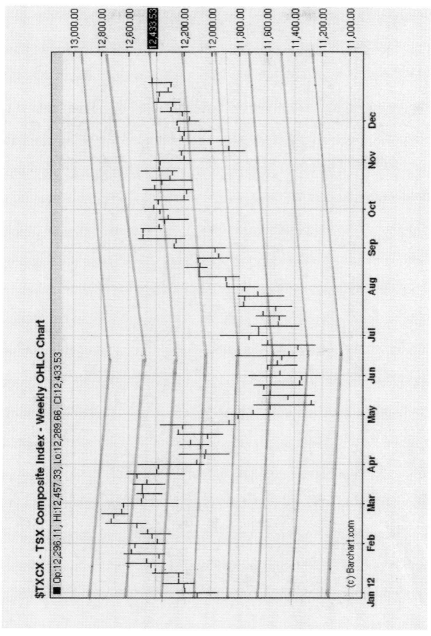

Figure 2-3 S&P TSX Composite Index weekly chart with
Saturn transit lines

Jupiter Transit Lines

Let's repeat this exercise, using the Euro Currency and Jupiter as an example.

The first step is to prepare the spreadsheet. In 2012, the Euro traded in a range of about 1.2000 to 1.3500. Consider starting the bottom part the spreadsheet at a value of 1.2000 and using increments of 0.0005 to craft the rows and columns. Table 2-4 illustrates what the first several columns of the spreadsheet should look like.

1	2	3	4	5	6
25	26	27	28	29	30
49	50	51	52	53	54
73	74	75	76	77	78
97	98	99	100	101	102
121	122	123	124	125	126
145	146	147	148	149	150
169	170	171	172	173	174
193	194	195	196	197	198
217	218	219	220	221	222
241	242	243	244	245	246
265	266	267	268	269	270
289	290	291	292	293	294
313	314	315	316	317	318
337	338	339	340	341	342

1.2	1.2005	1.201	1.2015	1.202	1.203
1.2165	1.217	1.2175	1.218	1.2185	1.2195
1.233	1.2335	1.234	1.2345	1.235	1.236
1.2495	1.25	1.2505	1.251	1.2515	1.2525
1.266	1.2665	1.267	1.2675	1.268	1.269
1.2825	1.283	1.2835	1.284	1.2845	1.2855
1.299	1.2995	1.3	1.3005	1.301	1.302
1.3155	1.316	1.3165	1.317	1.3175	1.3185

Table 2-4 Euro currency 2012 spreadsheet construction

Table 2-5 provides a Jupiter positional data point taken from the Ephemeris selected at the mid-month point for each month of 2012.

Month	Saturn Position at mid-Month	360 degree Equivalent
January	1 degree Taurus	31 degrees
February	4 degrees Taurus	34 degrees
March	9 degrees Taurus	39 degrees
April	16 degrees Taurus	46 degrees
May	23 degrees Taurus	53 degrees
June	1 degree Gemini	61 degrees
July	6 degrees Gemini	66 degrees
August	12 degrees Gemini	72 degrees
September	15 degrees Gemini	75 degrees
October	16 degrees Gemini	76 degrees
November	13 degrees Gemini	73 degrees
December	9 degrees Gemini	69 degrees

Table 2-5 Jupiter positional data for 2012

Table 2-6 shows the data points that should have been generated from the spreadsheet.

Month	360 degree Equivalent	Data Point	Data Point	Data Point	Data Point	Data Point	Data Point	Data Point	Data Point
January	31 degrees	1.203	1.219	1.236	1.252	1.269	1.285	1.302	1.318
February	34 degrees	1.204	1.221	1.237	1.254	1.270	1.287	1.303	1.320
March	39 degrees	1.207	1.223	1.240	1.256	1.273	1.289	1.306	1.322
April	46 degrees	1.210	1.227	1.243	1.260	1.276	1.293	1.309	1.326
May	53 degrees	1.218	1.235	1.251	1.268	1.284	1.301	1.317	1.334
June	61 degrees	1.222	1.239	1.255	1.272	1.288	1.305	1.321	1.338
July	66 degrees	1.225	1.241	1.258	1.274	1.291	1.307	1.324	1.340
August	72 degrees	1.228	1.244	1.261	1.277	1.294	1.310	1.327	1.343
September	75 degrees	1.234	1.250	1.267	1.283	1.300	1.316	1.333	1.349
October	75 degrees	1.234	1.250	1.267	1.283	1.300	1.316	1.333	1.349
November	73 degrees	1.216	1.233	1.249	1.266	1.282	1.299	1.315	1.332
December	69 degrees	1.210	1.226	1.243	1.259	1.276	1.292	1.309	1.325

Table 2-6 Jupiter data as obtained from the Euro currency spreadsheet

For each month in Table 2-6, plot the eight data points on a weekly chart of the Euro Currency futures. I have completed this exercise using a chart generated from www.barchart.com. The result is shown in Figure 2-4. What this chart with Jupiter transit lines reveals is intriguing. The Jupiter transit lines actually correspond to areas of support and resistance during the 2012 calendar year for the Euro Currency futures. As an interesting exercise, you can calculate the various data points for the 2013 calendar year. With these data points in hand, you now have a glimpse of what to expect for the Euro futures in 2013. Once again, this will leave you with insight that the vast majority of traders do not have.

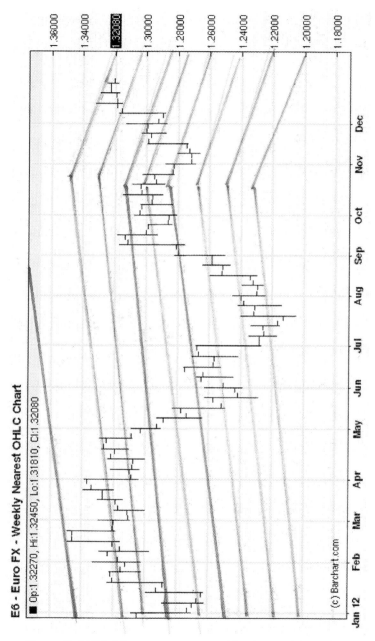

Figure 2-4 2012 Euro currency weekly chart with Jupiter transit lines

Saturn and Jupiter transit lines overlaid on price charts of stocks and commodities can give powerful insight as to support and resistance levels. These transit lines are calculated by converting planetary longitudinal positions into price using the Wheel of 24. Consider also using Uranus transit lines and Mars transit lines. Make careful note of where various transit lines intersect with each other.

CHAPTER THREE

Mathematics is the language with which God wrote the Universe.
Galileo Galilei—scientist, philosopher, mathematician
1564-1642

Square Roots, the Square of Nine and Gann Lines

When discussing with market enthusiasts the subject of applying esoteric mathematics to trading, I am repeatedly asked about Gann's *Square of Nine*. The Square of Nine exemplifies square root mathematics. The square root of a number 'a' is a number 'y' such that y x y = a. For example, the square root of 16 is 4. If one multiples 4 by itself (4 x 4) the result is 16.

The notion of square roots was well understood by civilizations dating as far back as the ancient Egyptians. W.D. Gann was likely introduced to the Square of Nine concept during his travels in Egypt or India. He did not invent the Square of Nine, but rather used it successfully in his trading. Hence to call it Gann's Square of Nine is misleading. It should simply be called the Square of Nine.

Building the Square of Nine

The Square of Nine is a spiral of numbers expressed on a 2-dimensional grid. The spiral of numbers starts from an apex and then spirals outwards in a clock-wise fashion. The starting apex point for the Square of Nine is the number one. From this starting point, add 1 to each successive number as you travel clockwise.

There are very expensive software programs available to help you generate very elegant Squares of Nine. To date, I have avoided buying such programs, opting instead for the elegant simplicity of a Microsoft Excel spreadsheet. The diagram in Figure 3-1 illustrates the basic construct of a Square of Nine. I have stopped my construct after I hit 361, but when building a square of Nine, one can certainly continue spiralling outwards for many more iterations.

45 degrees   90 degrees   135 degrees

307	308	309	310	311	312	313	314	315	316	317	318	319	320	321	322	323	324	325
306	241	242	243	244	245	246	247	248	249	250	251	252	253	254	255	256	257	326
305	240	183	184	185	186	187	188	189	190	191	192	193	194	195	196	197	258	327
304	239	182	133	134	135	136	137	138	139	140	141	142	143	144	145	198	259	328
303	238	181	132	91	92	93	94	95	96	97	98	99	100	101	146	199	260	329
302	237	180	131	90	57	58	59	60	61	62	63	64	65	102	147	200	261	330
301	236	179	130	89	56	31	32	33	34	35	36	37	66	103	148	201	262	331
300	235	178	129	88	55	30	13	14	15	16	17	38	67	104	149	202	263	332
299	234	177	128	87	54	29	12	3	4	5	18	39	68	105	150	203	264	333
298	233	176	127	86	53	28	11	2	1	6	19	40	69	106	151	204	265	334
297	232	175	126	85	52	27	10	9	8	7	20	41	70	107	152	205	266	335
296	231	174	125	84	51	26	25	24	23	22	21	42	71	108	153	206	267	336
295	230	173	124	83	50	49	48	47	46	45	44	43	72	109	154	207	268	337
294	229	172	123	82	81	80	79	78	77	76	75	74	73	110	155	208	269	338
293	228	171	122	121	120	119	118	117	116	115	114	113	112	111	156	209	270	339
292	227	170	169	168	167	166	165	164	163	162	161	160	159	158	157	210	271	340
291	226	225	224	223	222	221	220	219	218	217	216	215	214	213	212	211	272	341
290	289	288	287	286	285	284	283	282	281	280	279	278	277	276	275	274	273	342
361	360	359	358	357	356	355	354	353	352	351	350	349	348	347	346	345	344	343

0 degrees 360 (left)   180 degrees (right)

315 degrees   270 degrees   225 degrees

Figure 3-1 The Basic Construct of the Square of Nine

Support and Resistance using the Square of Nine

There is a great deal of confusion amongst traders and investors as to what the Square of Nine is all about. One does not really need a Square of Nine printout sitting on their desk as they study the markets. What is more important is a good understanding of the mathematical relationships between the numbers in the Square of Nine. The following paragraphs attempt to illustrate these relationships.

Take a number that you have spotted within the Square of Nine. Take the square root of that number. To this figure, add 0.25. Re-square the resulting sum and round to the nearest whole number. Look at where the result places you in the Square of Nine. Now, repeat this exercise, this time adding 0.5 instead of 0.25. Look at where the result places you within the Square of Nine. Numbers within the square of Nine are related to each other by square root mathematics. Continue to repeat this simple exercise adding 0.75, 1.0, 1.25, 1.50 and eventually 2.0. When it comes to adding 2.0, you will notice that the resulting outcome has taken you on one complete journey around the Square of Nine.

Let's now work an example. Locate the number 11 in the Square of Nine. The number 11 is situated on a horizontal axis called the 0 degree axis that projects from the number 1. The number 1 is the starting point of the Square of Nine. The square root of 11 is 3.3166. Add 0.25 to get 3.5666. Squaring this resulting number gives 12.72, which when rounded to the nearest whole integer gives 13. Take a look at where the number 13 is situated in relation to 11. It is situated on a 45 degree axis that projects from the number 1, the starting point of the Square of Nine.

Continuing on with the use of the number 11, take its square root and add 0.50 to get 3.8166. Square this number and you get 14.56. Rounding up to the nearest whole integer gives 15. The number 15 is situated on a 90 degree axis that projects from the number 1, the starting point of the Square of Nine.

Now take the square root of 11 and add 0.75. Re-square the result and you get 17 when rounded up to the nearest whole integer. Look at where 17 is located. It is on the 135 degree axis that projects out from the starting point of the Square of Nine.

Take the root of 11 and add 1.0. Re-square the resulting sum and you get 18.63. Round upwards and you get 19 which is located on the 180 degree axis that projects out from the starting point of the Square of Nine.

Take the root of 11 and add 1.5. Re-square the result to get 23.19. Rounding to the nearest integer gives 23 which is located on the 270 degree axis that projects out from the starting point of the Square of Nine.

Lastly take the square root of 11 and add 2. Re-squaring and rounding gives 28. The number 28 is situated on a horizontal axis called the 0 degree axis that projects from the number 1.

So, by taking the square root of a number, adding successively higher increments (0.25, 0.50. 0.75, 1.0, 1.25, 1.50 or 2.0) and re-squaring the result, one can navigate a full 360 degrees around the Square of Nine.

> Taking the square root of a number, adding 2 and re-squaring the result will take you on a complete journey around the Square of Nine. This principle is the key to using square root mathematics to determine resistance and support levels.

As I noted at the outset, the Square of Nine was not invented by Gann. The power of the square root was well understood by ancient civilizations. Gann merely made the connection between the mathematics of the square root and its harmony with the financial markets.

Traders and investors can follow in Gann's footsteps by using square root mathematics to get a sense of where resistance lines reside for a rising stock or commodity. The Square of Nine can also be used in reverse to determine where lines of support may reside in a falling market. For a given number on the square, take its root, subtract 0.25, 0.50, 0.75, 1.0, 1.25, 1.5 or 2. Re-square the result and round to the nearest integer. See where you end up on the Square.

To make matters easy for yourself, you can construct an Excel spreadsheet to do these square root calculations for you. Set the spreadsheet up so that once you input a price, the spreadsheet uses 0.25, 0.50, 0.75, 1.0, 1.25, 1.5 and 2 to calculate eight different outputs.

Figure 3-2 Resistance Levels for TSX: BB

Consider the following example. One stock that is very much in the news as I craft this manuscript is Research in Motion (TSX:BB), the challenged maker of the Blackberry smartphone. When this stock hit a low of $6.12 in September 2012, it was given up for dead. But, the chart in Figure 3-2 tells a very different tale. The various prices I have marked on the chart are the resistance levels calculated using Square of Nine methodology. To calculate these resistance levels, I did not actually build a Square of Nine. Rather, I put together a simple Excel spreadsheet where my starting point was $6.12. In my spreadsheet I expressed this value as simply 612 and followed the same methodology as I did in the previous paragraphs when I showed how to navigate around the Square.

Taking the root of 612 gives 24.7386. Adding 2 and re-squaring gives 714.95 which I rounded to 715 or $7.15. Look carefully at the left hand side of the chart and towards the end of September 2012, the share price actually encountered resistance at $7.12 before powering higher to test the $8.25 level. The level of $8.25 was calculated by taking the root of 612, adding 4 and re-squaring. The various other resistance levels marked on this chart were calculated in a like manner. At this time of writing, share price is

31

toying with resistance at $18.26 (root of 612 + 18, re-squared = $18.26). On January 21, 2013, TSX:BB reached an intraday high of $18.49 which is very close to the predicted $18.26.

From this intraday high of $18.49 which can be expressed as 1849, take the square root to get 43. Subtract 2 and square the result to get 1681 or $16.81. Repeating this method for several iterations eventually produces a result of 1225 or $12.25. In hindsight, we can see from Figure 3-2 that on January 31, 2013 TSX:BB found intra-day support at $12.17 which is very close to the calculated $12.25.

TSX:BB then rallied from this intra-day low of $12.17. Using this low which can be expressed 1217, take the square root and add 2. Square the result. Repeat this for several iterations. One number that will emerge as an overhead resistance level for the rally to run out of steam is $16.71. In fact, on March 14, we see that TSX:BB hit an intraday high of $16.41 on rumors that Chinese company Lenovo was going to make a takeover bid for this maker of Blackberry smart phones.

With a simple Excel spreadsheet to do these square root calculations, you can select a chart of your favorite stock or commodity futures contract, look for a significant high or low starting point and then quickly proceed to calculate expected resistance and support levels.

Square root mathematics is a scientific phenomenon that few market participants use or even understand. This chapter has now given you a comfortable understanding of support and resistance levels as calculated using square root mathematics. This valuable methodology can assist you in making more informed investment and trading decisions.

Gann Lines

The other subject that often comes up in discussion of esoteric math is that of Gann lines. I can recall a time when many financial market data providers had a Gann line function built into their charting software suites. Lately, I have noticed that this function does not appear as often as it once did. The reason for this, I suspect, is a general misunderstanding of Gann lines.

Gann lines are a technique in which a starting point of a significant high or low is selected. From this point, angles (vectors) are projected outwards. These vectors are the 1x1, 1x2, 1x4, 1x8 and the 2x1, 4x1 and 8x1. Some traders also use the 1x3 and 3x1 lines. The confusion with Gann lines comes from the scaling on the chart you are using. Ideally, the chart you are using must be constructed so that the height and width of the smallest increment on the chart has equal dimensions. Look carefully at most price charts and you will quickly see they are not constructed in this manner. In fact, look at the chart in Figure 3-2 and you will see that the one month increments of time on the horizontal axis are quite large compared to the smaller $1 increments of price on the vertical axis. Therefore, developing a computer function to automatically plot Gann lines is a challenge and this may be why many financial software platforms have abandoned Gann lines.

When plotting Gann lines, I thus prefer to create a chart in Microsoft Excel and plot my Gann lines manually. This way, I am sure I have done them correctly. To illustrate, Figure 3-3 presents a chart of Research in Motion (TSX:BB) price action covering the same time frame as in Figure 3-2. The starting point for extending Gann lines is the Sept 25th low of $6.12. I have created this chart in Microsoft Excel and then using a pencil and ruler added the Gann lines.

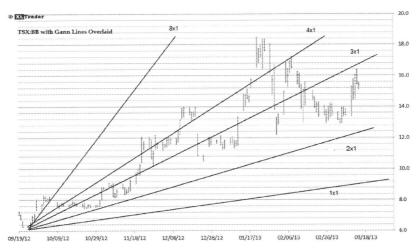

Figure 3-3 TSX: BB with Gann Lines

To create the Gann lines, the first step is to take the $6.12 low and express it as 612. Take the square root to get 24.73, add 1 and re-square to get 662 or $6.62. The difference between $6.62 and $6.12 is $0.50. This figure will be the increment for the y axis. The increment for the x axis is simply the square root of 612 or 24.73. So, to plot the 1x1 line, starting from the $6.12 low, one would go 24.73 calendar days (to October 19) along the x axis and up $0.50 on the y axis. The 2x1 line would be 49.46 calendar days (2 x 24.73) along the x axis and up $0.50 on the y axis. The various other lines would be plotted using the appropriate multiples.

From Figure 3-3, one can see that from the $6.12 lows, price action has encountered support and resistance along the various lines.

Another timely example is that of smartphone maker Apple which is very much in the news these days as I complete this manuscript. Apple (Nasdaq:AAPL) reached an all-time high of $705 on September 21, 2012. Using the same methodology as in the previous example, the root of 705 is 26.55. Hence, one unit of time on the horizontal axis is 26.55 days. Taking the square of 705, subtracting 1 and re-squaring gives us 652. The difference between $705 and $652 is $53. Hence, one increment on the y axis is $53.

The chart in Figure 3-4 illustrates price action of Apple shares with the 1x1 and 2x1 Gann lines overlaid. Despite the angst being expressed by the financial media over Apple's share performance, we can see from this chart that price action of AAPL is simply following the 1x1 Gann line as it seeks out a bottom in harmony with science and nature.

Figure 3-4 Nasdaq:AAPL with Gann Lines

The application of Gann Lines to a chart, when done properly using Square of Nine concepts, is a powerful tool that can help a trader see price action in a very different way.

I will conclude this chapter with one final example in which I have applied Gann lines from a price low and from a price high. I have also applied moving averages to demonstrate how more traditional technical analysis interacts with Gann lines. Figure 3-5 illustrates this application to the Philadelphia Gold and Silver Index ($XAU), known colloquially as the Gold Bugs Index.

Figure 3-5 Application of Gann Lines to the $XAU Index

The Index low selected for Gann line application was the 141 level from mid-May 2012. Using the square root methodology outlined in previous examples, the 1x1, 2x1, 4x1 and 8x1 lines were calculated. Notice how the 8x1 line corresponds to a crossover of the 20 and 50 day averages in July and again in November. The Index high selected for Gann line application was the 195 level from late-September 2012. Notice how the 8x1 line provided overhead resistance during the decline.

Gann lines are a technique in which a starting point of a significant high or low is selected. Using square root mathematics, angles (vectors) are calculated and projected outwards. These vectors are the 1x1, 1x2, 1x4, 1x8 and the 2x1, 4x1 and 8x1. Some traders also use the 1x3 and 3x1 lines.

Gann lines, constructed using square root mathematics, are a unique way to quantify the price behavior of stocks, commodity futures and market indices. This chapter has provided you with a working knowledge of how to create Gann lines and in so doing has provided you with a valuable tool to assist you in making better informed market decisions.

CHAPTER FOUR

*Time has no meaning in itself unless we choose to give it
significance*
Leo Buscaglia—author, speaker, professor
1924-1988

The New Year—January 1ˢᵗ or O degrees of Aries ?

In ancient Babylonian society, a year consisted of twelve lunar months. A lunar month was measured from one New Moon to the next. An astrologer or priestly seer would watch the night heavens and when a New Moon was spotted, he would announce that a new month had begun. Three times in every 19 years (a *metonic cycle*) an extra month was inserted to keep the calendar in general alignment with the seasons.

In 45 BC, Julius Caesar applied his understanding of astrology to the complexity surrounding having to add extra months. The result was the creation of the Julian calendar in which a year had 365.25 days. The Julian calendar represented an improvement over the Babylonian lunar calendar in that with the Julian system a calendar year differed only slightly from the actual length of a solar year (365.24 days). This meant that only once in every 131 years the Spring Equinox would be out of sync with the calendar by 1 year. To correct this discrepancy, on February 24, 1582 Pope Gregory XIII issued a papal decree ordering adoption of the Gregorian calendar.

The Gregorian calendar laid down some definitive rules for leap years and it determined that Easter would occur each year on the first Sunday after the first Full Moon after the Spring Equinox. The Gregorian calendar did not however define when a new year would start, although it is likely that Pope Gregory would have been comfortable with having a new year start at the Spring Equinox. By 1582, the general assumption amongst European society was that a new year started on January 1. To avoid unnecessary confusion, this practice was allowed to continue under the Gregorian calendar.

In North America we continue to start our new year on January 1. All too often then, when we are discussing the performance of a stock, an index or a commodity futures contract we describe it in terms of what it has done 'so far this year' or what it did 'last year'.

Must we examine a stock or a commodity using the man-made January 1 as the start of a new year? W.D. Gann answered this question when he designed a plotting construct that has come to be called the *Gann Box*. This construct uses a starting point of March 20 which is the date when the Sun is at 0 degrees of Aries. Sun at 0 degrees Aries is also what is called the Spring Equinox. Moving 3 months forward places the Sun in the sign of Cancer. This is called the Summer Solstice. Another 3 months forward places the Sun in the sign of Libra. This is the Autumn Equinox. Another 3 months forward places the Sun in Capricorn which denotes the Winter Solstice. One more increment of 3 months and the Sun is back to 0 degrees of Aries where its journey begins anew.

When plotting price data using this methodology, it is best to use weekly price data. On the sheet of graph paper used to construct a price chart, draw one weekly price bar (high-low) per one increment along the x axis. Next, divide the plot using a series of diagonal lines as illustrated in Figure 4-1. Notice how this configuration is divided into 4 segments according to the Solstices and Equinoxes.

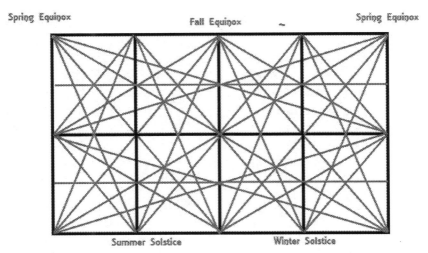

Figure 4-1 Configuration for a 0 Degrees Aries Plot

Figure 4-2 is a weekly chart of the $XAU Index (Philadelphia Gold and Silver Index) commencing from the week of March 20, 2011, the 0 degrees Aries point. The weekly price data was obtained from the Yahoo finance website (http://finance.yahoo.com) and plotted using high-low price bars on a simple piece of graph paper with one increment of the x axis being 1 week of time. The y axis was structured with a total height of 80 units to take into account the price range of $XAU (171 to 229) over the ensuing 52 weeks. When plotting in this manner, try to select an even number for the y dimension to make the plotting exercise as easy as possible. With the data plotted, use a ruler and a pen to draw in the various diagonal lines as per the example in Figure 4-1.

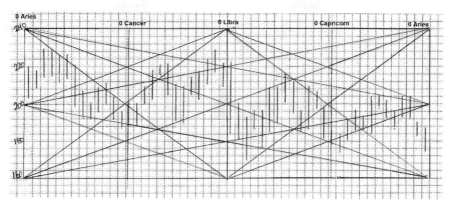

Figure 4-2 Weekly Plot of $XAU from
0 degrees Aries in March 2011

You have probably already observed how the various diagonal lines in Figure 4-2 provide support and resistance at various times of the year. This is definitely a unique way of looking at weekly price data. By employing this method of charting which blends equinoxes and solstices with price action, you may find that it gives you a unique perspective on price behavior.

Plotting data on graph paper is a time consuming exercise to be sure. Thankfully, there is an affordable option. I have discovered a vendor in the USA that sells an add-on function for Microsoft Excel that will produce the same chart as in Figure 4-2 with a lot less work. The add-on function is called XL Trader and it is available from http://Technical-Analysis-Addins.com. The cost of this add-on function is about US$40. It is straightforward to install and with a little practice easy to master. XL Trader comes equipped with applications to do various types of charting including hexagon grids. There is also a series of other add-on functions that can be purchased to do a variety of esoteric mathematical tasks including the planetary transit lines. I urge you to check out what is available.

Figure 4-3 illustrates the weekly chart of the $XAU Index prepared using the XL Trader add-in for Excel.

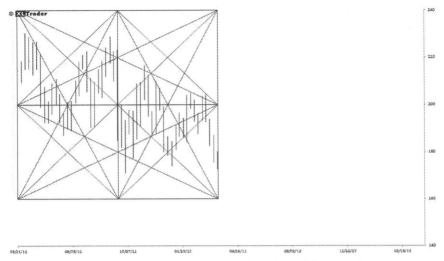

Figure 4-3 Weekly 0 degrees Aries Plot of $XAU using
XL Trader add-in for Excel

Instead of examining price action of a stock or commodity starting at January 1 of a year, consider a different view of price action using the Gann Box construct and a starting point of the Spring Equinox

CHAPTER FIVE

God used beautiful mathematics in creating the world
Paul Dirac—theoretical physicist
1902-1984

'M' and 'W' Chart Patterns

If the short term price trend of stocks, commodities or indices can change in response to emotion, are there certain esoteric patterns on price charts that traders and investors should be alert to?

W.D. Gann often receives credit for his ability to recognize unique appearing chart patterns. However, there is another individual that is equally deserving of credit. That individual is H.M. Gartley who was born in 1899 in New Jersey. At a young age Harold Gartley started working on the floor at the New York Stock Exchange and used his earnings to pay for his university studies eventually obtaining a Master's Degree in mathematics from New York University. Gartley went on to become a renowned trader on Wall Street. It is rumored he may even have known W.D. Gann and that they may have shared chart analysis information with each other.

Gartley noticed that price action for the stocks he traded on the New York Stock Exchange often exhibited distinct patterns.

AB=CD

One of the patterns Gartley noted was what he called the AB=CD pattern. Figure 5-1 illustrates the AB=CD pattern construct. This pattern starts from a distinct high or low price point on the chart. This high or low point is denoted point A. From point A, price will advance to point B and then pull back to point C. After point C, price will advance again to D in such a manner that the price range from A to B will equal the price range from C to D. This is why it is said AB=CD. These price ranges can be measured using low to high prices or close to close prices or sometimes a combination of both. I say this because price patterns on stocks or commodities do not always unfold with precision. When using patterns such as AB=CD, a small degree of flexibility is required on your part.

AB=CD pattern, in which leg AB is equal in size to leg CD

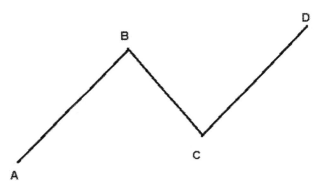

Figure 5-1 The Gartley AB=CD Pattern

Figure 5-2 Daily Chart of March 2013 Rice Futures

Figure 5-2 is a daily chart of Rice futures (March 2013 contract) in which the AB=CD pattern can be seen. The early-October 2012 high defines the A point, the November low the B point, the early December high the C point and the early January 2013 low the D point. In this pattern, on a close to close basis, the difference between A and B is 101 points (a $2020 move). On a high to low basis, the difference between C and D is 100 points. As noted, when watching for the AB=CD pattern, one must afford the market some flexibility because chart patterns do not unfold with exactitude. In this Rice example, both close to close and high to low price ranges are used when identifying the AB=CD pattern. An alert trader waiting for price to bottom so as to buy Rice futures would have seen price on leg CD pass through the level 0.382 x BC. He or she would have seen price pass through 0.618 x BC and then 0.786 x BC. He or she then would have started watching for an AB=CD pattern to unfold using a shorter term 15 minute chart to spot the turn in trend shortly after point D made itself apparent. With the change in trend spotted, he or she would have taken a long position in Rice futures. This sounds easy. The reality is, AB=CD patterns are not all that common. The patience required to sit and watch price action unfold is enormous. However, AB=CD patterns should be watched for and when identified, acted upon.

2-2-2 Patterns

Gartley also advanced variants of the AB=CD pattern which he called the 2-2-2 patterns. Both variants were discussed starting on page 222 of his 1935 classic *Profits in the Stock Market*. Author and trader Ross Beck claims that Gartley only published 1000 copies of his book and that he was selling copies for up to $1500 each in 1935 when the cost of a new Ford car in New York City was about $500. This would be the equivalent today of paying around $60,000 for a technical analysis trading book when an average car retails for around $20,000. If this is true, then Gartley was definitely held in high esteem by those Wall Street traders dedicated to technical chart analysis and esoteric math.

Figure 5-3 illustrates the buy and sell variants of the 2-2-2 pattern. Gartley assigned some strict rules to these patterns. Gartley noted that in order for these patterns to be valid, BC must be related to leg AB by a ratio of phi (Φ). Furthermore, he stated that point C cannot exceed point A and that point D must exceed point B. In the pattern illustrated at left in Figure 5-3, a trader would buy at point D. Observe how this pattern takes on the shape of the letter 'M'. In the pattern illustrated at right in Figure 5-3, a trader would sell at point D. Observe how this pattern takes on the shape of the letter 'W'.

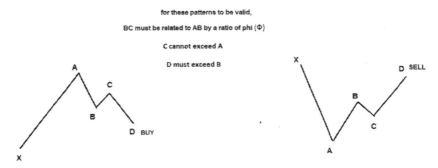

Figure 5-3 The Gartley 2-2-2 patterns

Over the years, many traders and authors have added twists and turns to the original Gartley approach. For example, veteran trader and author, Larry Pesavento has refined the Gartley 2-2-2 pattern with the notion that the price move A-D will be related to the price move between X and A by a phi (Φ) ratio.

Beck has introduced the parallelogram overlay in which points A-B-C-D and used to build a parallelogram. Recall from high school geometry class that a parallelogram is a shape in which opposing sides are parallel, opposing sides are equal in dimension and opposing angles are equal.

Beck has also addressed the psychological aspect of using the Gartley approach. As Beck points out in his 2010 book *The Gartley Trading Method*, it is fine to comment after the fact that traders *would have, could have and should have* followed a Gartley pattern.

It is quite another thing to see a Gartley pattern unfolding in real time and to have the patience to wait, the conviction to put on a trading position at the right time and the courage to take a modest profit without being overwhelmed by greed or by a market that suddenly turns around on you to erase trading gains.

I could not agree more.

Following Gartley's death in 1972, the original 1935 manuscript of *Profits in the Stock Market* was purchased from his widow. The manuscript was eventually sold to Lambert Gann Publishing who resurrected Gartley's ideas again when they re-released his 1935 classic. However, there seems to be some inconsistencies in content between the original edition of his book and the version released by Lambert Gann. I bought a copy of the Lambert Gann version for my personal collection from an on-line book retailer, only to find out it is not the same *Profits in the Stock Market* that I had the good fortune to study at the British Library in London in early 2013. The manuscript I studied in London actually discussed the AB=CD and 2-2-2 patterns whereas the edition I ordered from the on-line retailer contained different subject matter entirely.

Figure 5-4 Potash Corp (TSX: POT) and the Gartley 2-2-2
Buy Pattern

Figure 5-4 is a daily chart of Potash Corporation price action as seen on the Toronto Stock Exchange. This stock trades on both New York and Toronto Stock Exchanges. As per the Beck approach, the 2-2-2 pattern is overlaid on price charts using a shape called a parallelogram. From point A, a relative high, a line is drawn until it hits B. Another line is projected until it hits C. After that the rest is as simple as drawing parallel lines to complete the parallelogram shape and to derive point D. In this example, the move A through D on a close to close basis is related to the move X through A (close to close) by a ratio of 1.2. The square root of phi (Φ) is 1.29 which says that the Golden Mean is at work with price action on TSX:POT.

Notice how the construct of the parallelogram produces point D which aligns almost exactly with the November 2012 lows. Such is the elegance of the Gartley method and phi (Φ) mathematics. Point D according to the Gartley 2-2-2 method would have been a buying point. And as the chart shows, buying at point D would have resulted in a considerable profit as the stock moved higher towards the $44 level.

For another example, consider the case of Uranium. As of early 2013, there is much debate raging as to the future of Uranium as an energy source in light of the massive amounts of cheap shale gas currently being extracted around the globe. Uranium Participation Corp (TSX:U) is an appropriate proxy for Uranium as its main asset is a physical inventory of Uranium. Price action of this stock measures sentiment towards Uranium as a fuel source.

Figure 5-5 is a daily chart of TSX:U. In this chart, the price leg BC is related to AB by a ratio of 0.40 which is very close to 0.382 which is $1/\sqrt{\Phi 4}$. Do not expect ratios of price legs to align with pinpoint precision to phi (Φ) as markets will not correlate to phi (Φ) on three decimal points of precision. A close match is all you need to validate the pattern. In Figure 5-5 observe also that AD is related to XA in ratio of 0.80 using closing prices which is very close to 0.786 which is $1/\sqrt{\Phi}$.

I have further sketched a parallelogram to align with points A, B and C. It projects out to point D. As price was rising from point C, a trader following this method would have been wondering just what ratio of phi (Φ) was going to represent the stop of the price rally and the creation of point D. The parallelogram helps to answer this question. It projects out to the point in time where price should peak. And herein is another critical point. When using the parallelogram construct, price and time will not always meet up with one another exactly at point D. You have to be aware of the possible price targets based on the various phi (Φ) ratios of the leg XA and be alert to where the parallelogram positions point D. In Figure 5-5, price action peaked without having reached all the way to the apex of the parallelogram.

Figure 5-5 Gartley 2-2-2 Method and TSX:U

As another example, consider the case of Crude Oil. In Figure 5-6, leg BC (calculated using closing price data) is related to leg AB (calculated using high-low price data) by 0.60 which is very nearly 0.618. It is important that a trader using this method keeps an open mind and is flexible in the calculation of ratios when determining the validity of the pattern. Esoteric math does not always operate on pin-point precision. The price distance between

A and point D is related to leg XA by a ratio that very closely approaches 0.786. At point D, a trader may have entertained taking profits on existing long positions. He may also have taken a short position or even bought at the money put options. Notice in this Crude Oil example that the parallelogram construct is not on the chart. It is not always necessary to draw it. It is more important to ensure the Gartley pattern rules are met and to then use ratios of phi (Φ) to identify the D point in the pattern.

Figure 5-6 Gartley 2-2-2 Method and Crude Oil futures

Next, let's look at the e-mini Dow futures on a weekly basis going back to the 2009 lows. In Figure 5-7, I have denoted the March 2009 lows as point A. The price range XA is related to price range AD by 0.81, a close approximation to 0.782 given that we are dealing with weekly data. The parallelogram I have overlaid gives a hint where to expect point D to occur. Thus, traders looking for D to manifest itself would have had to exercise patience. From D, notice how the e-mini Dow futures sold off for a considerable trading gain for a trader with a short position.

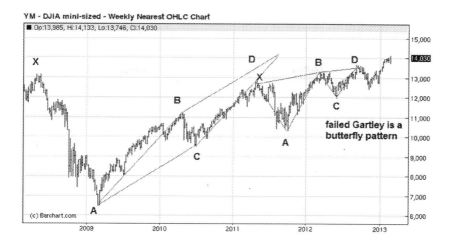

Figure 5-7 A Failed Gartley pattern

Pattern Failures

Re-labelling point D as point X allows us to now look for another Gartley setup with point A being the late 2011 lows and point C being the June 2012 lows. But, this is where something goes wrong and the pattern breaks down. After point A, price continues to rally such that point B exceeds that of point X. A key rule for the validity of a Gartley has now been violated. In the case of a pattern failure, one can calculate the price spread between X and A. The price spread between X and D may turn out to be related to X-A by a ratio of phi (Φ). The first ratio to be alert for is 1.272. Other ratios to watch are 1.618 and 2.058. In Figure 5-7, price action fails as price approaches a point so that XD = 1.30(X-A), a close match to 1.272. Seeing this development, one could go short the e-mini Dow, but as noted above this takes a certain level of conviction, given that the original 2-2-2 pattern has failed. Note how points X, A, B, C and D have been joined by line segments. XAB and BCD look like a pair of wings and indeed if you study the Gartley patterns beyond the scope of this book, you will come across the expression *butterfly pattern* or *bat pattern*. These patterns are nothing more than failed Gartley patterns. When studying the markets and charts, I tend to avoid failed Gartley patterns, opting instead to find another stock or commodity exhibiting a proper pattern. Should you choose to follow a failed bat or butterfly pattern, caution is warranted.

Gartley 2-2-2 patterns are not just the domain of daily and weekly charts. Figure 5-8 is a 60 minute chart of the March 2013 Australian Dollar futures. The classic 'W' pattern can be spotted on this chart. Leg XA is 106 ticks in size. On a close-close basis, leg AD is 85 ticks. AD is in proportion to XA in the ratio of 0.80 which is very close to 0.786. Hence, point D is a buy. Note that shortly after point D, there is a price bar that took a dangerous dip lower. This was nothing more than the market trying to flush out tight stop loss orders.

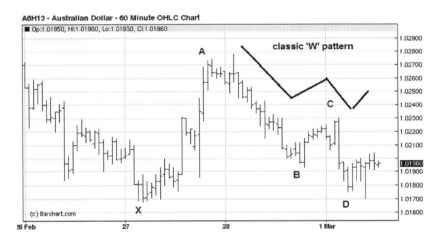

Figure 5-8 Australian Dollar—
Gartley Pattern on a 60 minute chart

Gartley 2-2-2 patterns can also be seen on longer term monthly charts too. Figure 5-9 is a monthly chart of the Japanese Yen futures price action (monthly nearest contract). I find this chart interesting because it exhibits a classic failed Gartley pattern. From the low in 1990, tracing out the A-B-C-D points shows that the low in 2002, which was point D, did not fall below point B. Therefore the pattern was a failure. However, when a pattern failure is encountered, do not turn your back forevermore on the stock or commodity in question. Keep watching its price action for a proper pattern to eventually form. In the case of the Yen, it took several years for a proper pattern to emerge on the monthly chart. Using the 2007 low as point X, points A, B and C can then be identified. Point D will conclude when D is at such a level that distance AD is related to XA by a ratio of phi (Φ). For AD = 0.618(XA), point D projects to the 1.01 level. For AD=0.786(XA), point D projects to 0.925. Clearly, the Yen is on a course towards further weakness under the monetary policy of the Abe government elected in February 2013.

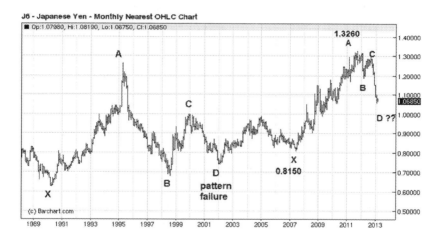

Figure 5-9 Gartley Pattern and the Japanese Yen

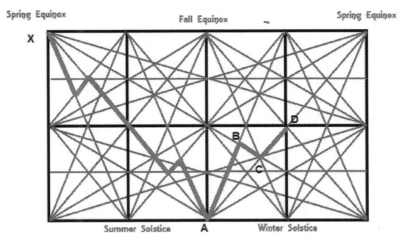

Figure 5-10 Gann Box meets Gartley method

I will conclude this chapter with one more thought for your consideration. Chapter 4, presented an alternative plotting method, oftentimes called the Gann Box. Figure 5-10 again shows the Gann Box, where I have further overlaid a second pattern along with labels X, A, B, C, D. Look familiar? This is the Gartley pattern overlaid on the Gann Box. If using the Gann Box for charting, be alert for the occurrence of Gartley patterns within it.

AB=CD and 2-2-2 patterns with their well- defined rules and their relationships to the mathematics of phi (Φ) are powerful tools for traders and investors to embrace. Proper use of these patterns can give traders and investors a significant edge.

CHAPTER SIX

Three things cannot long be hidden: the Sun,
the Moon and the Truth
Confucious—Chinese Philosopher
551-479 BC

The Power of the Moon

Look skyward on any clear night and you will see the Moon in one of its various phases. The Moon is the closest of all the planetary bodies to the Earth and has long been held in fascination by mankind. Chapter One made reference to the Moon with a discussion of Carolan's Spiral Calendar approach. In this Chapter, I delve further into the power of the Moon.

Throughout the centuries, the Moon has been associated with changing mood or health. In 6th century Constantinople (modern day Istanbul, Turkey), physicians at the court of Emperor Justinian advised that gout could be cured by inscribing verses of Homer on a copper plate when the Moon was in the sign of Libra or Leo. In 17th century France, astrologers used the Moon to explain mood changes in women. In 17th century England, herbal remedy practitioners advised people to pluck the petals of the peony flower when the Moon was waning. During the Renaissance period, it was thought that dreams could come true if the Moon was in the signs of Taurus, Leo, Aquarius or Scorpio.

Although some of these prescriptions now seem farcical, the Moon does continue to be recognized as a powerfully influential celestial body. There exists a fascinating correlation between the Moon and financial market behaviour. When used in combination with technical chart analysis, lunar phenomena can add a whole new dimension to trading certain stocks. This chapter examines Full and New Moon lunar phases and how they relate to short term changes of trend on certain stocks. This chapter also looks at the North Node of the Moon and its influence on markets as it changes signs of the zodiac. The relation between lunar phenomena and stock price behavior is a fascinating one. Just as the gravitational pull of the Moon can influence the action of tides, it somehow also influences our emotions of fear and hope. As our emotions of fear and hope change, our investment buying and selling decisions also change. The tangible result is a change in price trend action.

Lunar Phases and the Synodic Month

Much like the planets orbit the Sun, the Moon orbits the Earth. The Moon orbits the 360 degrees around the Earth in a plane of motion called the lunar orbit plane. This orbit plane is inclined at about 5 degrees to the ecliptic plane of the Earth. The Moon orbits Earth with a slightly elliptical pattern in approximately 27.3 days, relative to an observer on a fixed frame of reference like the Sun. This is known as a *sidereal month*. However, during one sidereal month, an observer located on Earth (a moving frame of reference) will revolve part way around the Sun. To that observer, a complete orbit of the Moon around the Earth will appear longer than the sidereal month at approximately 29.5 days. This 29.5 day period of time is known as a *synodic month* or more commonly a *lunar month*.

To an observer located on planet Earth, the Moon can be seen making various angles or phases to the Sun as the Earth journeys around the Sun. In fact, there are eight such phases of the Moon that astrologers work with. The New Moon occurs when the Moon is 0 degrees (or conjunct) to the Sun. The Crescent Phase occurs at a Sun-Moon angle of 45 degrees. The First Quarter Moon is at 90 degrees. The Gibbous Phase is at 135 degrees. The Full Moon is at 180 degrees. The Disseminating Phase is at 225 degrees. The Last Quarter Phase is at 270 degrees. The Balsamic Phase is at 315 degrees. For an excellent read on lunar phases, consider *Business Astrology 101* by Georgia Stathis.

When considering the Moon in the context of the financial markets, the two most impactful phases are the New Moon (0 degrees to the Sun) and the Full Moon (180 degrees to the Sun). Eclipses are also very potent events for market traders to be alert to. With an Ephemeris in hand one can easily identify when Full and New Moons will occur.

Full Moon, New Moon and the First Trade Date

The Moon has the greatest impact on those stocks that first traded (the *First Trade Date*) on a financial exchange during a Full Moon or a New Moon. Visit the website www.investingsuccess.ca and look for the navigation tab called **Astrology** and the sub-tab called **First Trade Dates**. Once a stock's First Trade Date is known, look up that date in an Ephemeris and see whether it coincides with either a Full or a New Moon. If the First Trade Date does align with a New or Full Moon, then that stock is a good candidate for a lunar trading strategy. To help you get started, Table 6-1 lists some stocks that had their First Trade dates on a New or Full Moon.

Company	Ticker Symbol	First Trade Date	Lunar Influence
Central Fund	TSX: CEF.a	June 14, 1965	Full Moon
Corby	TSX: CDL.a	February 3, 1969	Full Moon
Cdn. Western Bank	TSX: CWB	May 14, 1984	Full Moon
Calian Technology	TSX: CTY	September 15, 1993	New Moon
Cinram	TSX: CRW.un	March 10, 1986	New Moon
Mullen Group	TSX: MTL	December 13, 1993	New Moon
Manulife	TSX: MFC	September 24, 1999	Full Moon
Pan Am Silver	TSX:PAA	October 9, 1984	Full Moon
Power Corp	TSX: PWF	October 10, 1984	Full Moon
Toromont	TSX: TIH	May 21, 1974	New Moon
West Fraser	TSX: WFT	May 7, 1986	New Moon
WestJet	TSX:WJA	July 12, 1999	New Moon
American Express	N: AXP	May 18, 1977	New Moon
Caterpillar	N:CAT	December 21, 1929	New Moon
Citigroup	N:C	December 4, 1998	Full Moon
Duke Energy	N:DUK	July 12, 1961	New Moon
Fed Ex	N:FDX	December 28, 1978	New Moon
General Electric	N: GE	May 27, 1956	Full Moon

Honeywell	N:HUN	September 19,1929	Full Moon
JP Morgan	N:JPM	April 1, 1969	Full Moon
Lockheed Martin	N:LMT	March 16, 1995	Full Moon
Merck	N: MRK	May 15, 1946	Full Moon
Nabors	N:NBR	November 3, 2005	New Moon
Tyson Foods	N:TSN	October 17, 1997	Full Moon

Table 6-1 Lunar First Trade dates for several
Canadian and US listed companies

Consider the example of heavy equipment maker Caterpillar which trades on the New York Stock Exchange under the ticker N:CAT. Caterpillar made its debut onto the New York Stock Exchange on December 21, 1929, the date of a New Moon. The daily chart in Figure 6-1 illustrates the price action of Caterpillar for a nine month period commencing in May 2012. Circled areas denote Full Moons while squared areas denote New Moons. Note the alignment of New and Full Moon occurrences to price gaps and to swing highs and swing lows. When using lunar events as part of a trading strategy watch price action one or two days ahead of the lunar event. Consider also using shorter term charts to zero in on changes of trend.

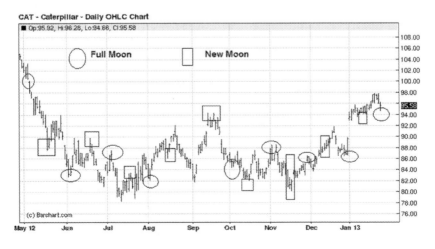

Figure 6-1 Caterpillar (N:CAT) daily chart

While there is only one Full Moon and one New Moon per month, these events nonetheless are powerful especially for stocks that have an affinity for lunar events as a result of a First Trade being on a New Moon or Full Moon. To further illustrate the point, consider the example of conglomerate General Electric which trades on the New York Stock Exchange under the ticker N:GE. General Electric made its debut onto the New York Stock Exchange on May 27, 1956, the date of a Full Moon. The daily chart in Figure 6-2 illustrates the price action of General Electric for a nine month period commencing in May 2012. Circled areas denote Full Moons while squared areas denote New Moons. Once again, the alignment of price swings to New and Full Moon occurrences is riveting.

Figure 6-2 General Electric (N:GE) daily chart

Stocks having a first trade date on either a full Moon or New Moon will very often exhibit short term trend changes on Full Moon and/or New Moon dates.

The North Node of Moon

The Earth orbits the Sun in a plane called the ecliptic. The Moon orbits the Earth in its own plane called the lunar orbit plane. Mathematically, two planes that are not parallel must intersect. The intersection points between the Moon's plane and Earth's ecliptic are termed the North and South nodes. Astrologers tend to focus on the North node and Ephemeris tables will clearly list the zodiac position of the North Node for each calendar day. Study the North Node positions and you will see that it moves in a backwards, retrograde pattern through the zodiac. The length of time for the North Node to make a full journey through the 12 signs of the zodiac is 18.6 years.

As part of a trading or investing strategy, consider noting the times when the North Node changes signs of the zodiac, approximately every 1.55 years. The chart in Figure 6-3 illustrates monthly price behaviour of the S&P500 Index dating back to 1998. On the chart, the circled areas depict the times when the North Node changed signs of the zodiac. Note how these times of sign change align closely with pivotal swing highs and lows including the market peak in 2000 and the peak that preceded the financial crisis of 2008. The North Node moved into the sign of Scorpio on August 29, 2012 and several weeks later the S&P500 Index crested and began to decline as debates over the US 'fiscal cliff' intensified. The North Node will remain in the sign of Scorpio until February 2014. In the February 2014 timeframe, be alert for a notable trend change in the markets.

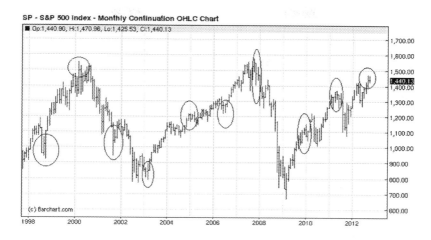

SP - S&P 500 Index - Monthly Continuation OHLC Chart
■ Op:1,440.90, H:1,470.96, Lo:1,425.53, Cl:1,440.13

(c) Barchart.com

Figure 6-3 S&P500 Index—North Node changing signs

The North Node and the Business Cycle

In 1938, author and trader Louise McWhirter published her *Theory of Stock Market Forecasting*. One of the more fascinating sections of her book deals with the general business cycle and the North Node of the Moon. She posits that the general economy will move in a 19 year business cycle in harmony with the 18.6 year synodic period of the North Node which can be seen to move in a backwards retrograde motion through the zodiac from our vantage point here on Earth. As the North Node moves into the sign of Taurus, the general economy will slow down. This below normal economic behavior will last for about 3 years until the Node passes out of the sign of Aquarius which is considered to be the bottom of the 19 year cycle. Interestingly in late 1928 the Node transited into Taurus which signalled a slowdown. Some nine months later, the stock market crashed and a harsh economic climate set in. As the Node moves through Capricorn and Sagittarius, the economy will pick up momentum again. Through Scorpio and Libra, the general economy will approach a very high level of activity with a peak in activity coming as the Node leaves the sign of Leo. As the Node then moves through the signs of Cancer and Gemini, economic activity is positive but beginning to slow to more normal levels. Of course, the caveat to this cycle behavior is external political and socioeconomic events that may arise unexpectedly.

Real estate analysts and economists who follow the rigors of astrology, have noted that this business cycle behavior can be seen in the real estate market, not just in the USA but globally. In 2006, global real estate markets peaked in terms of re-sale price and overall demand. In June 2006, the Node moved into the sign of Pisces. In December 2007, the Node moved into the sign of Aquarius, an indication of a low point in economic activity. In reflection, late 2007 through late 2008 while the Node was in Aquarius was indeed the darkest hour for the global real estate industry and for the global economy in general. The Node entered Scorpio in late August 2012. While the economy is by no means on solid footing yet and the real estate market is not what it once was, it is easy to see that a marked improvement has been made as measured by job creation data and housing data. Although not shown here, the US Home Construction ETF (N:ITB) bottomed between late 2009 and late 2012 as the Node moved through Sagittarius and into Capricorn. Barring any major upsets with Euro-zone cohesiveness or stability in other parts of the globe, the general economy should continue to improve until the Node transits out of Leo in late 2018. To follow global real estate developments in the context of this Node cycle, I recommend an Australian website created by economist Phillip Anderson, www. businesscycles.biz.

The North Node of Moon changing signs can be seen to align with trend changes on the markets. The journey of the North Node through the 12 zodiac signs aligns with the general economic business cycle.

Solar and Lunar Eclipses

A solar eclipse occurs when the Moon passes between the Sun and Earth and fully or partially blocks the Sun. This can happen only at a New Moon, when the Sun and the Moon are in conjunction and only when the New Moon occurs close to one of the Nodes. Because the Moon's lunar orbit plane intersects with the ecliptic plane at the two Nodes that are 180 degrees apart, New Moons occur close to the nodes at two periods of the year approximately six months (173.3 days) apart, known as *eclipse seasons*. There will always be at least one solar eclipse during an eclipse season. Sometimes the New Moon occurs close enough to a node during each of two consecutive months to eclipse the Sun in two partial eclipses. This means that in any given year, there will always be at least two solar eclipses, but there could be as many as five.

A lunar eclipse occurs when the Sun, Earth, and Moon are aligned exactly, or very closely so, with the Earth in the middle. The Earth blocks the Sun's rays from striking the Moon. This can only happen at a Full Moon. Eclipse dates should be watched for closely as price trend changes often can occur at these times. The chart in Figure 6-4 illustrates monthly price behaviour of the S&P500 futures dating back 15 years. The circles on the chart depict many of the solar and lunar eclipse dates. Notice how these dates align quite well with swings in price action. Appendix A provides Full Moon, New Moon and eclipse data for 2013 through 2014. Traders and investors following eclipse events could consider using technical chart analysis to study price action of stocks and commodity futures as eclipse dates approach. Any oversold or overbought conditions that could lend themselves to a trend reversal at the eclipse, can then be acted upon accordingly.

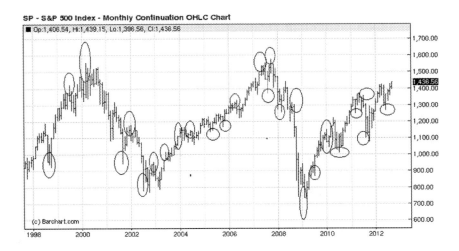

Figure 6-4 S&P500 Index—Solar and Lunar eclipses

As an example, the chart illustrated in Figure 6-5 is an hourly snapshot of the Dow Jones Industrial Average around the time frame of June 4, 2012, the date of a partial lunar eclipse and the date of a market swing low. A trader seeking to enter a trade on Dow futures could have watched the developing technical negative divergence and the rising ADX feature to time an entry position.

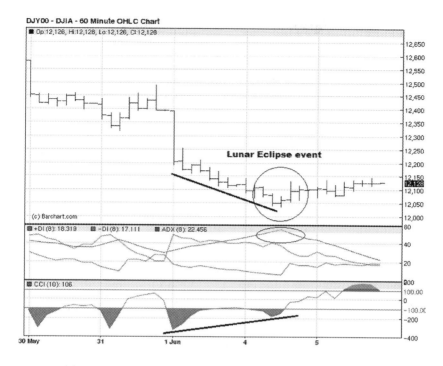

Figure 6-5 Dow Jones Industrial Average hourly chart

Volatility and the Moon

In 2004 the Chicago Board Options Exchange created a derivative instrument to measure the implied volatility of S&P500 Index options. This instrument has become very popular with both traders and the media alike and it is most often referred to by the name 'VIX'. At any given time, what the VIX tells the observer is the expected volatility on the S&P Index for the following 30 days. For example, if the VIX has a reading of 15 on a particular day, then traders should expect the S&P500 Index to exhibit volatility of $15/\sqrt{12} = 4.33\%$ over the following 30 days. The impact of the Moon can be seen when studying the VIX. Figure 6-6 is a daily chart of VIX price action from late 2012 to March 2013. New Moon events and Full Moon events have been marked on this chart. Traders with short term time horizons may be interested to notice that the VIX tends to increase in value between the time of a New Moon and a Full Moon.

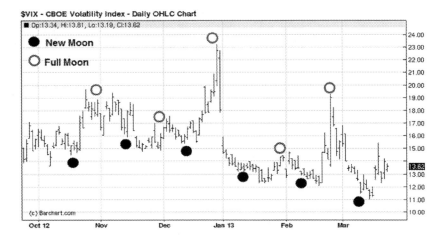

Figure 6-6 Lunar Events and the VIX

Market volatility as measured by the CBOE VIX tends to increase from the time of a New Moon to the time of a Full Moon.

CHAPTER SEVEN

The cosmos is a vast living body, of which we are still parts. The sun is a great heart whose tremors run through our smallest veins. The moon is a great nerve center from which we quiver forever. Who knows the power that Saturn has over us, or Venus? But it is a vital power, rippling exquisitely through us all the time.

D.H. Lawrence-novelist, poet, playright
1885-1930

The Planets Know . . .

There are eight planets that are important to the application of astrology to trading and investing on the financial markets. These planets are Mercury, Venus, Mars, Jupiter, Saturn, Uranus, Neptune and Pluto.

In my previous book, *The Bull, the Bear and the Planets*, I provided a wide ranging look at many of the planets and their aspects with one another. I showed how these aspects aligned to trend changes on equity markets and on commodity futures.

This chapter looks at how synodic periods between the outer planets (Mars, Jupiter, Saturn and Uranus) can be incorporated into a trading strategy. Synodic periods between pairs of these planets can be seen to align with 10 year, 7 year, 5 year and 2 year market cycles going back many decades. This chapter concludes with a look at synodic periods of Mercury with these outer planets as well as synodic periods of Venus with these outer planets. These Mercury and Venus synodic periods can be seen to align to 3 month and 7 month market cycles respectively.

The Power of Attraction

The diagram in Figure 7-1 (courtesy of www.zoomschool.com) shows the positional arrangement of the planets in relation to the Sun. Note the sizes of the other planets in comparison to Earth. In 1687 Isaac Newton contemplated the attraction between two masses. In 1798 scientist Henry Cavendish took Newton's work and examined it in the context of the two masses being planetary bodies. He further quantified the notion of a gravitational constant which then led to the expressing of Newton's Law of Attraction as:

$$G = (m1\ m2)/\ r^2$$

where G is equal to 6.674×10^{-11} N m^2/kg^2, m1 and m2 are the masses of two planetary bodies and r is the distance of separation of the two planetary bodies.

In other words, the attraction between two planetary bodies is related to the product of their masses and varies inversely as the square of the distance between them. In the case of planet Earth, even though Jupiter, Saturn and Uranus are distantly removed (which would reduce the gravitational attraction), the product of the mass of Earth times the large mass of any one of these large bodies will compensate to still result in a mathematically significant force of attraction. Thus, from an esoteric viewpoint, it seems reasonable to speculate that these larger outer planets do exert a force of attraction on Earth which in turn can affect our emotions which in turn can affect our buying and selling decisions on the markets.

Figure 7-1 The Planets

Synodic Cycles

Each of the different planets takes a different period of time to complete a full revolution around the Sun. Table 7-1 shows these different periods of revolution. Mercury being the closest planet to the Sun, completes its journey very quickly in only 88 days. Pluto on the other hand, being very far away from the Sun, takes a good long while to complete its orbit in 245 years.

Planet	Time to Orbit Sun
Mercury	88 days
Venus	225 days
Earth	365 days
Mars	687 days
Jupiter	11.85 years
Saturn	29.42 years
Uranus	83.75 years
Neptune	163.74 years
Pluto	245.33 years

Table 7-1 Time for an Orbit around the Sun

A synodic cycle is that length of time for a celestial body to complete an entire pattern as referenced from a fixed observation point being the Sun. Such a pattern is usually taken to mean the time from when a planet is conjunct (0 degrees) to another planet to when it is again conjunct that other planet.

Table 7-2 presents various planet to planet synodic cycles. A synodic cycle between two planets is given by S = (s1 x s2)/(s2-s1), where s1 and s2 are the times to orbit the Sun as taken from Table 7-1 previous.

	Earth	Mercury	Venus	Mars	Jupiter	Saturn	Uranus	Neptune	Pluto
Mercury	116 days		144.5 days	100.9 days	89.8 days	88.7 days	88.2 days	88.1 days	88.0 days
Venus	584 days	144.5 days		334.5 days	237.3 days	229.8 days	226.6 days	225.8 days	225.5 days
Mars	780 days	100.9 days	334.5 days		2.23 years	2.0 years	1.92 years	1.90 years	1.90 years
Jupiter	399 days	89.8 days	237.3 days	2.23 years		19.85 years	13.81 years	12.77 years	12.45 years
Saturn	376 days	88.7 days	229.8 days	2.0 years	19.85 years		45.26 years	35.68 years	33.40 years
Uranus	370 days	88.2 days	226.6 days	1.92 years	13.81 years	45.26 years		171.42 years	127.15 years
Neptune	367 days	88.1 days	225.8 days	1.90 years	12.77 years	35.68 years	171.42 years		492.34 years
Pluto	367 days	88.0 days	225.5 days	1.90 years	12.45 years	33.40 years	127.15 years	492.34 years	

Table 7-2 Planet-Planet Synodic Cycles

Financial astrologers have long focused on the 19.85 year Jupiter-Saturn synodic cycle. As noted above, the masses of these two large bodies are such that the effect of their gravitational pull on Earth should not be readily dismissed as a factor influencing human emotion and the markets.

Heliocentric Ephemeris tables show that Jupiter and Saturn were roughly 0 degrees separated from early 1901 to early 1902. The slow moving nature of these bodies means that angular aspects between them will take many months to complete. Data also shows that from mid-1910 through early 1912, Jupiter and Saturn spent time 180 degrees separated. Jupiter and Saturn were 90 degrees separated during the periods mid 1905 through mid-1906 and early 1916 through early 1917.

Figure 7-2 is a chart of the Dow Jones Industrial Average from 1900 to 1920. Each of these Jupiter-Saturn timeframes has been marked on this chart. You may have already spotted that each of these timeframes was associated with topping action on the Dow Jones Average. Alert traders at the time who were using astrology likely benefitted handsomely.

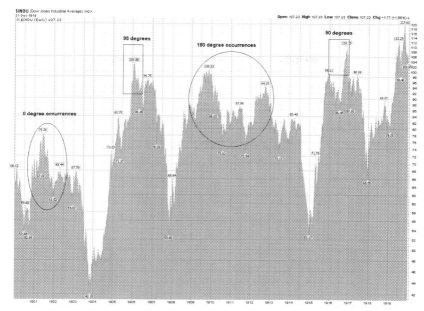

Figure 7-2 Dow Jones Industrial Average 1900 to 1920
with Jupiter-Saturn aspects

But, there is another way of looking at this chart, or any longer term chart for that matter—and that is to look for distances between significant trend changes to align with moves such as 120 degrees of Saturn, ½ of a Saturn-Jupiter cycle, 30 degrees of Uranus or 60 degrees of Saturn. Even shorter cycles such as the Mars-Saturn synodic period can be important.

Before delving into these cycles, it is interesting to examine the history of bodies such as Uranus, Saturn, Jupiter and Mars.

Mars

Mars is periodically visible from Earth with its reddish hue. To the Babylonians, Mars was the God of war and pestilence. To the Greeks, it was called Ares and was also associated with war. The Romans also linked Mars with war and celebrated the festival of

Mars in early springtime from whence our month of March derives its name.

Saturn

At various times of year, Saturn is visible from Earth. Ancient Greek and Roman astronomers were able to align its appearances to their belief systems. To the Greeks, Saturn was one of the many children of Gaia, Mother Earth, and Uranus, the sky god. Uranus was not a committed partner and out of frustration Gaia sent her son Saturn to kill him. This explains why astrologers regard Saturn as the bringer of law, order, time and cycles. To the ancient Romans, Saturn was the god of seed sowing, time and harvest. The first recorded observations of Saturn using a telescope are credited to Galileo Galilei in 1610.

Jupiter

Jupiter is also visible from Earth. To the ancient Greeks, Jupiter was the God Zeus. To the Romans, Jupiter was the son of Saturn. When Saturn devoured his children, only Jupiter survived. Hence, Jupiter is regarded even today as the planet of luck and positive influence. The first recorded observations of Jupiter's moons are credited to Galileo Galilei in 1610.

Uranus

As telescope technology improved towards the late 1700s, astronomers could see farther into space. The discovery of planet Uranus in 1781 is credited to English astronomer William Herschel.

Uranus requires about 84 years to complete an entire trip around the zodiac and thus spends about 7 years in each zodiac sign. Astrologers regard Uranus as the planet of inventions, change, breakthroughs and wars.

Regarding the times for planets to advance and to make cycles, think of these time spans as building blocks. As you look at longer term charts, apply these building blocks in repetitive sequences and you will start to see how they can explain market behaviours.

Using the synodic data from Tables 7-1 and 7-2, we can delineate some key times to use as building blocks as shown in Table 7-3. Appendix B provides a short refresher on how to use an Ephemeris to obtain the times for these building blocks.

Synodic Cycle or Planetary Advancement	Time
Saturn-Uranus cycle	45.26 years
½ of a Saturn-Uranus cycle	22.63 years
¼ of a Saturn-Uranus cycle	11.31 years
Jupiter-Saturn cycle	19.85 years
½ of a Jupiter-Saturn cycle	9.92 years
Jupiter-Uranus cycle	13.81 years
½ of a Jupiter-Uranus cycle	6.9 years
Jupiter-Neptune cycle	12.77 years
½ of a Jupiter-Neptune cycle	6.38 years
120 degree move of Saturn	9.8 years
60 degree move of Saturn	4.9 years
30 degree move of Uranus	6.97 years
Mars-Saturn cycle	2.0 years

Table 7-3 Cycles and Advancements

Figure 7-3 displays the same chart of the Dow Jones Industrial Average from 1900 to 1920 as in Figure 7-2. The chart in Figure 7-3 has been overlaid with several of the building blocks from Table 7-3. Think about the traders in the early 1900s who followed the markets with the aid of their Ephemeris tables. They clearly had a distinct advantage over those traders who were unaware of astrology altogether.

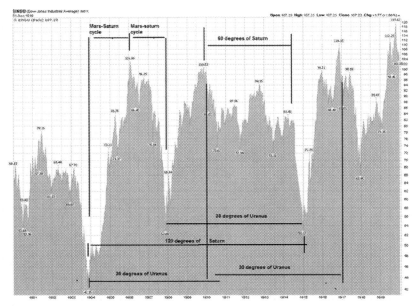

Figure 7-3 Dow Jones Industrial Average
1900 to 1920—Saturn, Uranus and Mars

Figure 7-4 is a chart of the Dow Jones Industrial Average from 1920 to 1939. This period is most infamous for the events of 1929 that saw a disastrous crash on Wall Street. The 1929 Crash did not materialize out of thin air. It appears to have come at the mid-point of a Saturn-Jupiter cycle that got underway in late 1919 at a significant market high (see right hand side of Figure 7-3). In fact, the entire market rally that culminated in the Crash of 1929 started in 1921. The time from the start of this rally to the Crash and then to the ultimate bottom is very closely that of one of Jupiter's cycles around the Sun. From the 1932 low to the peak of the ensuing recovery rally is a time very closely equated to a 60 degree advancement in the movement of Saturn.

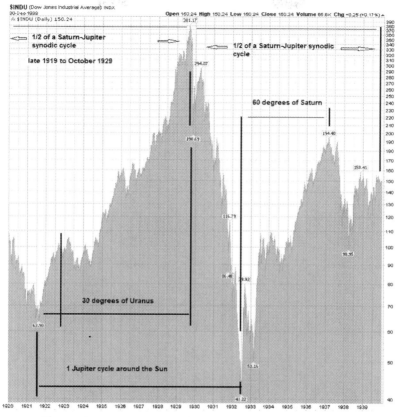

Figure 7-4 Dow Jones Industrial Average 1920 to 1939

Figure 7-5 is a chart of the Dow Jones Industrial Average from 1940 to 1960. This period was one of particular strength as the post-war economy recovered with the USA leading the way. Despite what appears to just be a market in a sustained uptrend, the planets are making themselves felt. From the 1932 market lows to the 1942 lows that preceded a sizeable rally is a time span best described as 120 degrees of Saturn. From the 1942 low to a minor low in 1949 is a time span related to 30 degrees of Uranus. Another time span of 30 degrees Uranus took the markets to a peak in 1956. Lastly, notice that after making a modest low in 1949, the markets rallied into 1960, a time span of 120 degrees of Saturn.

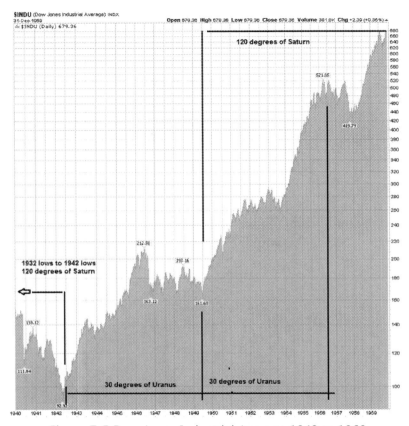

Figure 7-5 Dow Jones Industrial Average 1940 to 1960

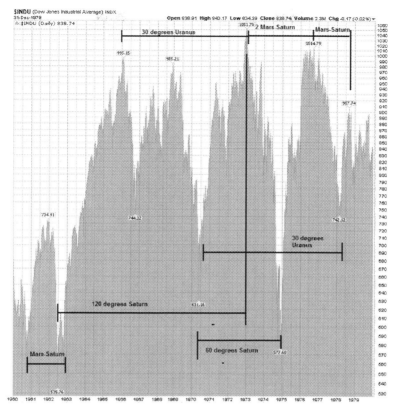

Figure 7-6 Dow Jones Industrial Average 1960 to 1979

Figure 7-6 is a chart of the Dow Jones Industrial Average from 1960 to 1979. Volatility had returned to the markets and to society in general during the time frame depicted on this chart. Rising inflation, the assassination of a President, the impeachment of another and a military action in Vietnam that was hugely unpopular with the masses all contributed to the turmoil of the time. I have marked several synodic cycles on this chart. With the aid of an Ephemeris you can likely spot cycles by piecing together some of the preceding Dow Jones charts. For example, is the time frame from the October 1929 highs to the early 1975 lows a full Saturn-Uranus cycle of 45.26 years?

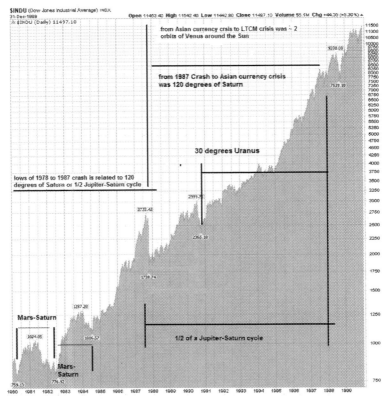

Figure 7-7 Dow Jones Industrial Average 1980 to 1999

Figure 7-7 is a chart of the Dow Jones Industrial Average from 1980 to 1999. The crash of 1987, when compared to other market downturns we have seen in recent years, now seems minuscule in proportion. Like other market sell-offs we have seen, the 1987 event did not just up and happen one day out of thin air It occurred after a time span of about 120 degrees Saturn had elapsed from the market lows in 1978. Following the 1987 event, markets picked themselves up and began to rally. One-half of a Jupiter-Saturn cycle later resulted in another crisis—the Asian Currency Crisis. From the Asian crisis, two solar orbits of Venus later, the markets hit another upsetting event—the failure of massive hedge fund Long Term Capital Management (LTCM). It is also interesting to note the time frame from the early 1975 low to the LTCM crisis corresponds very nearly to ½ of a Saturn-Uranus cycle.

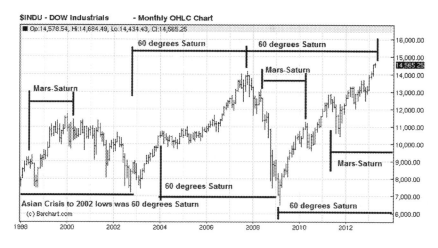

Figure 7-8 Dow Jones Industrial Average
1998 to early 2013

Figure 7-8 presents the performance of the Dow Jones Industrial Average from 1998 to early 2013. There are several observations we can piece together from looking at Figure 7-8. A Mars-Saturn cycle from the October 2011 lows will take us to about October 2013. A 60 degree advance of Saturn from the early 2009 lows takes us to late 2013 as well. From the highs in 2000, a Jupiter-Uranus cycle takes us to late in 2013 while a Jupiter-Neptune cycle takes us to early 2013. From the late 2007 highs, a move of 60 degrees Saturn takes us to early 2013. From the May 2011 highs, a Mars-Saturn cycle takes us to mid-2013. Early 2013 saw the start of a sizeable rally which reached all-time highs in mid-2013.

At this time of writing (early April 2013) I note the financial media is hugely optimistic towards the markets. A highly optimistic media combined with coming cycle completions is not a good thing according to my contrarian mindset. From the highs in September 2007, a move of 30 degrees Uranus takes us to near the summer of 2014. From the 2002 market lows, a Jupiter cycle of 11.85 years places us in mid-2014. So with a confluence of cycles ahead of us in a world beset with debt, banking crises and other problems, it is most definitely a good time to be a market trader with a comfortable grasp on financial astrology.

> Studying market price action using movements of 60 and 120 degrees of Saturn, 30 degrees of Uranus, the Jupiter-Saturn synodic cycle, the Mars-Saturn synodic cycle, Venus synodic cycles and the Mercury synodic cycles can provide unique perspectives.

The Seven Month Cycle

If one peruses financial market literature on cycles, the notion of a seven month cycle can be found often with little in the way of an explanation. The seven month cycle concept derives from the synodic cycle of Venus in relation to Jupiter (237 days), (Saturn 229 days), Uranus (226 days) and Neptune (225 days). Note that all of these time spans are very near to 7 calendar months in duration.

Figure 7-9 illustrates weekly price action of the S&P500 Index from late 2008 to March 2013. I have marked on the chart spans of time that are between 225 and 237 days. These spans of time represent the synodic cycles of Venus with one of Jupiter, Saturn, Uranus or Neptune. Observe how these spans of time align with swings in the market. This explains the popularity of the seven month cycle notion. The next time you see reference to this cycle in market literature, you will have a good understanding of how it is calculated.

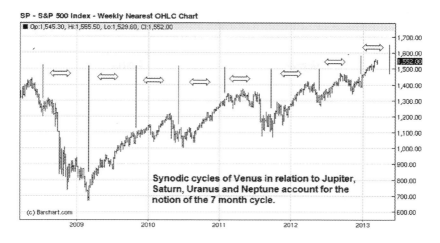

Figure 7-9 Synodic cycles of Venus and the
seven month cycle

The Three Month Cycle

Literature on market cycles may also contain references to what
traders call the three month cycle. The concept of the three
month cycle derives from the synodic cycles of Mercury with Mars
(100 days), Jupiter (89 days), Saturn (88 days), Uranus (88 days),
Neptune (88 days) or Pluto (88 days). Note that all of these time
spans are very near to 3 calendar months in duration.

Figure 7-10 illustrates weekly price action of the S&P500 Index
from late 2008 to March 2013. I have marked on the chart spans
of time that are between 88 and 100 days. These spans of time
represent the synodic cycles of Mercury with one of Mars, Jupiter,
Saturn, Uranus, Neptune or Pluto. Observe how these spans of
time align with swings in the market. This explains the popularity of
the three month cycle notion. The next time you see reference to
this cycle in market literature, you will have a good understanding
of how it is calculated.

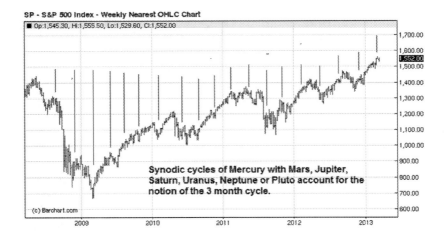

Figure 7-10 Synodic cycles of Mercury and the
three month cycle

CHAPTER EIGHT

*Behind it all is surely an idea so simple, so beautiful
that when we grasp it—in a decade, a century, or a
millennium—we will all say to each other, how could it
have been otherwise?*
John Archibald Wheeler-theoretical physicist
1911-2008

Gann Forecasts—Deciphering the Arcane

In the 1920s, W.D. Gann was noted for the annual market forecasts he provided to subscribers of his newsletter service. In the re-printed version of Gann's *Truth of the Stock Tape*, there is a copy of his 1929 forecast which he mailed to his subscribers in late 1928. In this forecast he breaks the coming year 1929 down into its respective months and for each month he lists certain dates that traders are advised to be alert to for possible market trend changes. Deciphering these dates proves to be an interesting exercise that combines planetary aspects, planetary sign changes and lunar astrology—all subjects discussed in this book as well as in my book *The Bull, the Bear and the Planets*. An analysis of Gann's 1929 forecast is a suitable way for me to conclude this book as his forecast illustrates how these astrological principles all work together.

There are two notions to keep in mind when looking at Gann's forecast work. From time to time celestial bodies will align with each other at positions of the zodiac so that 3 or more celestial bodies can be seen to create unique geometrical patterns. Figure 8-1 illustrates several of these patterns.

Also to keep in mind is the fact that my treatment of lunar astrology in this book has been mainly confined to a discussion of Full Moons, New Moons and eclipses. There are times of the month when the orbiting Moon will make aspect angles with the various planets. Gann focused intently on aspect angles of the Moon to Mercury, Venus and Mars. Gann further appears to have been mindful of aspects of the Sun to Jupiter, Saturn, Uranus, Neptune and Pluto.

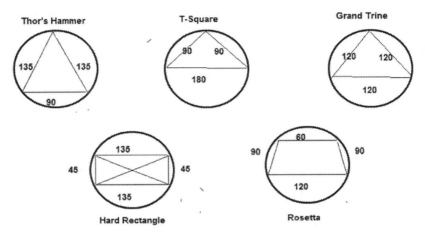

Figure 8-1 Patterns of Celestial Bodies

In Gann's 1929 forecast he noted the following dates as being important for changes of trend:

January 1929: 5th to 7th, 12th to 15th, 18th to 24th.

February 1929: 9th to 12th, 20th to 22nd, 27th to 28th.

March 1929: 10th to 11th (very important), 21st to 22nd (important), 28th to 29th (very important).

April 1929: 3rd, 9th to 10th, 13th to 15th, 21st to 23rd.

May 1929: 3rd to 4th (watch stocks that make tops at this time), 9th to 11th (watch for some stocks to make bottoms and for others to top), 22nd to 23rd, 29th to 31st (very important).

June 1929: 1st to 2nd (quite important), 7th to 10th (another important time), 21st to 23rd (a more important change).

July 1929: 3rd to 5th (very important for trend change), 9th to 10th (also quite important), 21st to 24th (more important).

August 1929: One of the most important months for change of trend. Many stocks will start on their long downtrend. 7th to 8th (quite important), 16th to 17th (important), 23rd to 24th (important), 29th to 20th (of minor importance).

September 1929: 2nd to 3rd (important), 16th to 17th (important—should be bottom of panicky decline), 21st to 24th (important for top), 27th and 28th (important for bottom of a big break).

October 1929: 2nd, 8th to 9th, 18th to 20th (very important—watch stocks that start to decline and go with them), 26th to 28th (of minor importance).

November 1929: 1st to 2nd, 10th to 22nd (a very important period for wide fluctuations), 17th to 19th and 24th to 25th.

December 1929: 1st to 2nd (important), 16th to 17th (of minor importance), 23rd to 24th (greater activity and of major importance).

In addition to unique geometrical formations and planetary aspects, Gann was also alert to the orbiting Moon making aspects with certain key points of the zodiac during each lunar month. These key points can be found in the natal chart of the New York Stock Exchange as illustrated in Figure 8-2.

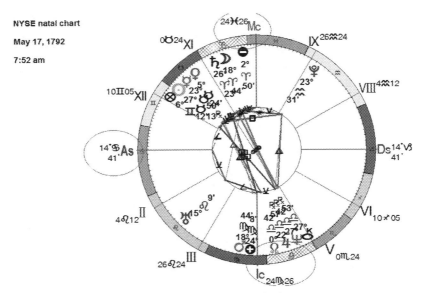

Figure 8-2 NYSE Natal Chart

The New York Stock Exchange enjoys a birthdate of May 17, 1792. In this natal chart, key points for Gann were the Mid-Heaven (MC) at 24 degrees of Pisces, the Ascendant (Asc) at 14 degrees of Cancer and the Immum Coeli (IC) at 24 degrees of Virgo. The 10th House of this natal chart straddles all of the sign of Aries and a small bit of Pisces. Mars is the ruler of Aries and Neptune is the ruler of Pisces. Therefore, Mars and Neptune were also key to Gann's analysis.

As an aside, this is where the work of Gann takes an interesting twist. In 1938, the technique of watching dates when the Moon made aspects to certain key points taken from the natal chart of the New York Stock Exchange was described in a book by Louise McWhirter entitled *McWhirter Theory of Stock Market Forecasting*. The question then becomes, who was Louise McWhirter? In my travels to complete research for this book, I came across no other books by Louise McWhirter and in fact found little mention of her at all. I find it more than curious that W.D. Gann was using this same technique in his 1929 forecast. In my humble opinion, Louise McWhirter was a pen name for someone else wishing to keep his identity a guarded secret. That someone may well have been W.D. Gann.

Table 8-1 takes Gann's 1929 date ranges and provides pertinent astrological information that was seen to be occurring at those times. Table 8-2 provides additional data. As you study Tables 8-1 and 8-2, you will likely come to the same conclusion that I have—W.D. Gann was extremely well versed in astrology and that is what gave him his edge over other traders in the markets. As to how and why the unique aspects and formations identified by Gann influenced market participant emotion—that question remains unanswered.

1929 Date Range	Celestial Body Changing Signs of Zodiac	Zodiac Patterns or Notable Aspects	Mercury and Moon	Venus and Moon	Mars and Moon	Moon Phase
January 5th-7th	Venus	Neptune, Moon, Venus, form a T-Square. Venus, Pluto, Moon approach a Thor's Hammer.		90 degree aspect		
January 12th-15th		Saturn, Neptune, Jupiter form a Grand Trine	0 degree aspect	0 degree aspect	90 and 120 degree aspects	NEW MOON
January 18th-24th	Sun	Mercury goes retrograde, Mars turns direct. Sun 90 degrees to Jupiter.	90 and 120 degree aspects	90 and 120 degree aspects	0 degree aspect	FULL MOON
February 9th-12th		Mars 45 degrees to Sun. Sun 45 degrees to Uranus.	0 degree aspect	0 degree aspect	90 and 120 degree aspects	NEW MOON
February 20th-22nd	Neptune	Saturn, Jupiter, Neptune approaching Grand Trine. Sun 180 degrees to Neptune.	180 degree aspect	90 and 120 degree aspects		FULL MOON

February 27th-28th		Moon, MC and Mars form a Grand Trine. Mars, Moon and Mercury form a Thor's Hammer.	90 degree aspect			
March 10th-11th	Mars	Saturn, Mars, Pars Fortune form a T-Square.			90 degree aspect	NEW MOON
March 21st-22nd		Saturn, Venus, Neptune approach a Grand Trine.		90 and 120 degree aspects		EQUINOX
March 28th-29th		Sun 0 degrees to Uranus. Moon, Mercury, Pluto making a Grand Trine.	120 degree aspect	180 degree aspect		
April 3rd	Mercury			90 degree aspect		
April 9th-10th			0 degree aspect	0 degree aspect	90 degree aspect	NEW MOON
April 13th-16th		Venus, Neptune, and Saturn form a Grand Trine.	90 degree aspect	90 degree aspect	0 degree aspect	
April 21st-23rd	Sun	Mercury, Neptune and Saturn form a Grand Trine. Sun 120 degrees Saturn.	180 degree aspect	180 degree aspect	90 degree aspect	FULL MOON
May 3rd-4th	Mercury Saturn		90 degree aspect			
May 9th-11th	Mars		0 degree aspect			NEW MOON / Eclipse
May 22nd-23rd		Saturn, Neptune, Venus approaching a Grand Trine.			90 and 120 degree aspects	FULL MOON/ Eclipse
May 29th-30th		Saturn, Neptune and Venus form the Grand Trine	120 degree aspect		180 degree aspect	
June 1st-2nd	Venus	Saturn, Neptune and Venus remain within a Grand Trine	90 degree aspect			
June 7th-10th		Saturn, Mars and North Node form a Thor's Hammer	0 degree aspect	90 degree aspect	0 degree aspect	NEW MOON

Date	Planet	Configuration				Moon Phase
June 21st-23rd	Sun	Uranus, Mars, Moon approach a Thor's Hammer.		120 degree aspect	120 degree aspect	FULL MOON / SUMMER SOLSTICE
July 3rd-5th	Mars		0 degree aspect	0 degree aspect	90 degree aspect	NEW MOON
July 9th-10th	Mercury	Pars Fortune, Mercury, and Saturn form a T-Square.		90 degree aspect	0 degree aspect	
July 21st-24th	Sun	Venus, Mars, Moon form a Thor's Hammer.	180 degree aspect	90 and 120 degree aspects	180 degree aspect	FULL MOON
August 7th-8th	Venus	Mars, Saturn, Venus form a T-Square.		90 degree aspect	0 degree aspect	
August 16th—17th		Moon, Venus and Uranus form a Grand Trine.	120 degree aspect	180 degree aspect	120 degree aspect	
August 23rd-24th	Sun	Saturn, Moon, Pluto and Mercury form a Rosetta.		90 degree aspect		
August 29th-30th		Uranus, Mars, Moon form a T-Square.	90 degree aspect		90 degree aspect	
September 2nd—3rd	Venus					NEW MOON
September 16th-17th		Mars, Moon, Jupiter Grand Trine.	120 degree aspect	180 degree aspect	120 degree aspect	FULL MOON
September 21st-24th	Sun, Venus	Moon, Venus, Saturn Grand Trine.	180 degree aspect	120 degree aspect	180 degree aspect	
September 27th-28th	Venus		90 degree aspect		90 degree aspect	
October 2nd			0 degree aspect			NEW MOON

Table 8-1 Analysis of Gann 1929 Forecast (cont'd)

1929 Date Range	Celestial Body Changing Signs of Zodiac	Zodiac Patterns or Notable Aspects	Mercury and Moon	Venus and Moon	Mars and Moon	Moon Phase
October 8th-9th	Mars	Moon, Jupiter, Venus form a T-Square.	90 degree aspect	90 degree aspect		
October 18th-20th	Venus Mercury turns Direct	Venus, Saturn, Node form a Thor's Hammer.	120 and 180 degree aspects	120 degree aspect	180 degree aspect	FULL MOON
October 26th-28th					90 degree aspect	
November 1st-2nd			0 degree aspect		0 degree aspect	NEW MOON / Eclipse
November 10th-22nd	Venus, Sun, Mars	Mercury, Pluto, Moon form a Grand Trine. Moon, Saturn and Pars Fortune form a T-Square. Moon, Node, Saturn form a Thor's Hammer.	180 and 120 degree aspects	90, 120, 180 degree aspects	90, 120, 180 degree aspects	FULL MOON / Eclipse
November 24th-25th			90 degree aspect		90 degree aspect	
December 1st-2nd	Saturn		0 degree aspect		0 degree aspect	NEW MOON
December 16th-17th		Neptune, Node, Mercury approach Grand Trine.	180 degree aspect		180 degree aspect	FULL MOON
December 23rd-24th	Sun		90 degree aspect		90 degree aspect	

Table 8-1 Analysis of Gann 1929 Forecast

1929 Date Range	Further Notable Aspects
January 5th-7th	Neptune 180 degrees to Venus, Sun 180 degrees to Pluto. Moon 120 degrees to MC. Moon 120 degrees to Asc. Moon 90 degrees to Neptune.
January 12th-15th	Mercury 135 degrees to Mars, Mercury 45 degrees to Saturn, both hard aspects. Moon 0 degrees Mercury. Moon at MC.
January 18th-24th	Mercury 120 degrees to Mars, Venus 90 degrees to Mars, Venus 45 degrees to Jupiter, Mercury 45 degrees to Uranus, Venus 120 degrees Pluto. Moon 90 degrees to Sun. Moon 0 degrees to Mars. Moon at Asc.
February 9th-12th	Mercury 45 degrees to Saturn. Moon 0 degrees Mercury. Moon 180 degrees Neptune. Moon at MC.
February 20th-22nd	Venus 90 degrees Pluto, Sun 135 degrees Pluto. Moon at Asc. Moon 0 degrees Neptune.
February 27th-28th	Sun 45 degrees Venus. Moon 120 degrees to Mars. Moon 90 degrees to Mercury.
March 10th-11th	New Moon. Moon at MC.
March 21st-22nd	Sun 90 degrees to Saturn. Moon 0 degrees Neptune.
March 28th-29th	Moon 45 degrees Saturn. Moon 120 degrees Mercury.
April 3rd	Mercury 90 degrees Saturn, Sun 135 degrees Neptune. Moon crosses Dsc.
April 9th-10th	Mercury 135 degrees Neptune. Mercury 90 degrees Mars. Moon 0 degrees Mercury.
April 13th-16th	Mars 0 degrees Pluto. Moon crosses Asc.
April 21st-23rd	Venus 120 degrees Neptune. Sun 0 degrees Venus. Moon 90 degrees Mars.
May 3rd-4th	Mercury 45 degrees Pluto, Mercury 90 degrees Neptune, Venus 90 degrees Mars. Moon 90 degrees Mercury.
May 9th-11th	Moon 0 degrees to Mercury.
May 22nd-23rd	Sun 90 degrees Neptune, 90 degrees Mars and 45 degrees Pluto. Moon 90 degrees to Mars.
May 29th-31st	Moon 180 degrees to Mars. Moon crosses Dsc.
June 1st-2nd	Moon at MC and 90 degrees Mercury.
June 7th-10th	Mercury 45 degrees Venus, Sun 0 degrees Mercury. Moon at Asc and 0 degrees Mercury.
June 21st-23rd	Sun transits through 180 degrees to Saturn. Moon 120 degrees Mars, 180 degrees Mercury, 120 degrees Neptune.
July 3rd-5th	Sun 90 degrees Uranus, Venus 45 degrees Uranus, Sun 45 degrees Neptune. Moon 0 degrees Mercury, 90 degrees Mars, 90 degrees Neptune.

July 9th-10th	Venus 90 degrees Neptune, Mercury 180 degrees Saturn, Venus 45 degrees Pluto, Sun 0 degrees Pluto. Moon 0 degrees Neptune, 0 degrees Mars and at Asc.
July 21st-24th	Mercury 0 degrees Pluto, Mercury 45 degrees Jupiter. Moon crosses Dsc, 180 degrees Mercury, 180 degrees Neptune.
August 7th-8th	Mercury 120 degrees Saturn. Moon 0 degrees Mars, at IC.
August 16th—17th	Mercury 90 degrees Jupiter, Sun 120 degrees Saturn. Moon 120 degrees Mars, 120 degrees Mercury, at the Dsc,
August 23rd-24th	Sun 0 degrees Neptune. Moon 180 degrees Mars and crosses MC.
August 29th-30th	Venus 45 degrees Jupiter. Moon crosses Asc, and is 90 degrees to Mars and Mercury.
September 2nd—3rd	Sun 0 degrees Jupiter. Mercury 0 degrees to Mars. Moon 0 degrees Neptune and at the IC.
September 16th-17th	Sun 90 degrees Saturn, Mercury 90 degrees Pluto. Moon 120 degrees Mars, 120 degrees Mercury and at the MC.
September 21st-24th	Moon 180 degrees Mars and Mercury.
September 27th-28th	Venus 0 degrees Neptune. Moon across Asc and is 90 degrees to Mars and Mercury.
October 2nd	Sun 180 degrees Uranus, Mercury 90 degrees Pluto.
October 8th-9th	Sun 120 degrees Jupiter, Sun 0 degrees Mercury, Venus 45 degrees Mars. Moon 120 degrees Neptune.
October 18th-20th	Mercury 180 degrees to Uranus, Venus 90 degrees Saturn. Moon 180 degrees Mars.
October 26th-28th	Venus 180 degrees Uranus, Mercury 120 degrees Jupiter, Mercury 45 degrees Neptune. Moon 90 degrees Mars and 0 degrees Neptune.
November 1st-2nd	Venus 120 degrees Jupiter and 45 degrees Neptune. Moon 0 degrees Mars.
November 10th-22nd	Mercury 45 degrees Saturn, Sun 0 degrees Mars, Sun 0 degrees Mercury, Sun 120 degrees Pluto and 135 degrees Uranus, Venus 135 degrees Jupiter, Mercury 120 degrees Pluto and 135 degrees Uranus. Moon crosses Asc and is 180 degrees Mars.
November 24th-25th	Sun and Mercury 90 degrees Neptune. Moon crosses IC and is 0 degrees Neptune.
December 1st-2nd	Sun 180 degrees Jupiter, Sun-Mercury-Mars are all 0 degrees apart in Sagittarius. Moon aspects these planets.

December 16th-17th	Mercury 120 degrees Neptune, Mercury 0 degrees to Saturn. Moon 180 degrees Mars and Mercury and crosses Asc.
December 23rd-24th	Sun, Saturn at 0 degrees to one another. Moon 90 degrees to Sun, 90 degrees to Mercury.

Table 8-2 Analysis of Gann 1929 Forecast (cont'd)

To assist you in seeing how Gann's forecast correlated to actual market behavior, Table 8-3 presents the daily price action of the Dow Jones Industrial Average for 1929. This data has been obtained from the St. Louis Federal Reserve Bank website. As you examine the data and the various dates in Gann's forecast, do not be too concerned about the absolute moves around these dates. Rather, focus on the percentage magnitude of the moves. As you see some of these percentages, think about how investors would react in today's markets to similar-sized percentage moves. For example, the period January 5th to 7th, 1929 was marked by a Mystic Rectangle, a Thor's Hammer, Venus square Moon and Sun opposite Pluto. During this brief time span, the Dow Jones average dropped 1.97 percent and then went on to recoup those losses in the four trading sessions that followed. As another example, the period March 21st to 22nd, 1929 was marked by a Thor's Hammer, the Spring Equinox and Sun square Saturn. This critical juncture then saw the Dow Jones Average drop by 6 percent over four trading sessions before levelling off.

After you have studied the data, I trust you will see why Gann was so motivated and enthused by the effects of astrology on the markets. In particular, I further draw your attention to Gann's prediction that September 2nd to 3rd, 1929 would be important. The astrological data shows that this timeframe was marked by a New Moon and aspects of Sun 0 degrees Jupiter and Mercury 0 degrees Mars. Mars figures prominently in first trade chart of the New York Stock Exchange dating to May of 1792. Gann also knew that unfavorable aspects to Mars at the time of a New Moon could cause significant stock market moves. This time span in September 1929 marked the price peak of the Dow Jones Industrial Average prior to its precipitous decline that is now referred to as the 'Crash of 1929'.

To help prepare Tables 8-1 and 8-2, I used a software program called Millenium Trax, distributed by AIR Software. Even with this program, it took me fair amount of time to examine all the astrological data for 1929. I cannot imagine how much work it must have been for W.D. Gann to compile the same data without the aid of a software program. The man is to be revered for his tenacity and dedication to applying astrology to the financial markets.

DATE	INDEX VALUE
1929-01-02	307.01
1929-01-03	305.72
1929-01-04	304.75
1929-01-07	297.70
1929-01-08	296.98
1929-01-09	300.83
1929-01-10	301.58
1929-01-11	301.66
1929-01-14	304.06
1929-01-15	297.66
1929-01-16	302.66
1929-01-17	303.95
1929-01-18	304.14
1929-01-21	304.64
1929-01-22	307.06
1929-01-23	310.33
1929-01-24	309.39
1929-01-25	315.13
1929-01-28	314.04
1929-01-29	312.60
1929-01-30	312.60
1929-01-31	317.51

1929-02-01	319.68
1929-02-04	319.05
1929-02-05	322.06
1929-02-06	317.18
1929-02-07	305.75
1929-02-08	301.53
1929-02-11	310.35
1929-02-13	308.07
1929-02-14	306.49
1929-02-15	300.41
1929-02-18	300.74
1929-02-19	301.10
1929-02-20	305.99
1929-02-21	310.06
1929-02-25	311.24
1929-02-26	311.25
1929-02-27	314.53
1929-02-28	317.41
1929-03-01	321.18
1929-03-04	313.86
1929-03-05	310.20
1929-03-06	305.20
1929-03-07	308.99
1929-03-08	311.59
1929-03-11	305.75
1929-03-12	306.14
1929-03-13	310.29
1929-03-14	316.26
1929-03-15	319.70
1929-03-18	317.59
1929-03-19	317.53
1929-03-20	316.44
1929-03-21	314.63
1929-03-22	310.26
1929-03-25	297.50
1929-03-26	296.51
1929-03-27	303.22

1929-03-28	308.85
1929-04-01	300.40
1929-04-02	303.49
1929-04-03	300.35
1929-04-04	305.37
1929-04-05	303.04
1929-04-08	301.49
1929-04-09	299.13
1929-04-10	300.67
1929-04-11	304.09
1929-04-12	305.43
1929-04-15	302.43
1929-04-16	304.19
1929-04-17	309.91
1929-04-18	311.87
1929-04-19	310.58
1929-04-22	315.33
1929-04-23	316.62
1929-04-24	315.66
1929-04-25	314.28
1929-04-26	314.15
1929-04-29	313.84
1929-04-30	319.29
1929-05-01	320.13
1929-05-02	321.52
1929-05-03	325.56
1929-05-06	326.16
1929-05-07	321.91
1929-05-08	323.51
1929-05-09	321.17
1929-05-10	325.70
1929-05-13	316.49
1929-05-14	320.79
1929-05-15	319.35
1929-05-16	320.09
1929-05-17	321.38
1929-05-20	312.70

1929-05-21	314.09
1929-05-22	300.83
1929-05-23	308.09
1929-05-24	305.64
1929-05-27	293.42
1929-05-28	298.87
1929-05-29	296.76
1929-05-31	297.41
1929-06-03	304.20
1929-06-04	310.57
1929-06-05	307.68
1929-06-06	307.72
1929-06-07	307.46
1929-06-10	303.27
1929-06-11	306.64
1929-06-12	306.68
1929-06-13	313.05
1929-06-14	313.68
1929-06-17	319.33
1929-06-18	319.67
1929-06-19	316.41
1929-06-20	317.73
1929-06-21	320.68
1929-06-24	321.15
1929-06-25	326.16
1929-06-26	328.60
1929-06-27	328.91
1929-06-28	331.65
1929-07-01	335.22
1929-07-02	340.28
1929-07-03	341.99
1929-07-05	344.27
1929-07-08	346.55
1929-07-09	345.57
1929-07-10	343.30
1929-07-11	343.04
1929-07-12	346.37

1929-07-15	341.93
1929-07-16	344.24
1929-07-17	345.63
1929-07-18	344.59
1929-07-19	345.20
1929-07-22	341.37
1929-07-23	345.48
1929-07-24	343.04
1929-07-25	344.67
1929-07-26	345.47
1929-07-29	339.21
1929-07-30	343.12
1929-07-31	347.70
1929-08-01	350.56
1929-08-02	353.08
1929-08-05	352.50
1929-08-06	351.39
1929-08-07	348.44
1929-08-08	352.10
1929-08-09	337.99
1929-08-12	351.13
1929-08-13	354.03
1929-08-14	354.86
1929-08-15	354.42
1929-08-16	361.49
1929-08-19	365.20
1929-08-20	367.67
1929-08-21	365.55
1929-08-22	369.95
1929-08-23	374.61
1929-08-26	374.46
1929-08-27	373.79
1929-08-28	372.06
1929-08-29	376.18
1929-08-30	380.33
1929-09-03	381.17
1929-09-04	379.61

1929-09-05	369.77
1929-09-06	376.29
1929-09-09	374.93
1929-09-10	367.29
1929-09-11	370.91
1929-09-12	366.35
1929-09-13	366.85
1929-09-16	372.39
1929-09-17	368.52
1929-09-18	370.90
1929-09-19	369.97
1929-09-20	362.05
1929-09-23	359.00
1929-09-24	352.61
1929-09-25	352.57
1929-09-26	355.95
1929-09-27	344.87
1929-09-30	343.45
1929-10-01	342.57
1929-10-02	344.50
1929-10-03	329.95
1929-10-04	325.17
1929-10-07	345.72
1929-10-08	345.00
1929-10-09	346.66
1929-10-10	352.86
1929-10-11	352.69
1929-10-14	350.97
1929-10-15	347.24
1929-10-16	336.13
1929-10-17	341.86
1929-10-18	333.29
1929-10-21	320.91
1929-10-22	326.51
1929-10-23	305.85
1929-10-24	299.47
1929-10-25	301.22

1929-10-28	260.64
1929-10-29	230.07
1929-10-30	258.47
1929-10-31	273.51
1929-11-04	257.68
1929-11-06	232.13
1929-11-07	238.19
1929-11-08	236.53
1929-11-11	220.39
1929-11-12	209.74
1929-11-13	198.69
1929-11-14	217.28
1929-11-15	228.73
1929-11-18	227.56
1929-11-19	234.02
1929-11-20	241.23
1929-11-21	248.49
1929-11-22	245.74
1929-11-25	243.44
1929-11-26	235.35
1929-11-27	238.95
1929-12-02	241.70
1929-12-03	249.61
1929-12-04	254.64
1929-12-05	251.51
1929-12-06	260.12
1929-12-09	259.18
1929-12-10	262.20
1929-12-11	258.44
1929-12-12	243.14
1929-12-13	249.60
1929-12-16	245.88
1929-12-17	249.58
1929-12-18	246.84
1929-12-19	240.42
1929-12-20	230.89
1929-12-23	232.65

1929-12-24	234.07
1929-12-26	240.96
1929-12-27	240.66
1929-12-30	241.06
1929-12-31	248.48

Table 8-3 Dow Jones Industrial
Average price data for 1929

Dates when either Full Moons, New Moons, eclipses, aspects between planets, aspects between the Moon and planets or unique aspect shapes between 3 or 4 planets combine can often be key times for changes of price trend. Dates when the Moon touches key parts of the New York Stock Exchange natal chart can also be times for price trend changes.

EPILOGUE

Final Thoughts

The financial markets are dynamic entities that reflect the mass psychology of traders and investors. The forces of nature that exist in our cosmos influence this mass psychology. Scientific phenomena including square root mathematics, numerical sequences, lunar events, planetary transits and planetary aspects can be seen to correlate to these emotional changes and to trend changes in the financial markets.

In the early years of the 20th century the most successful traders on Wall Street, including the venerable W.D. Gann and the mysterious Louise McWhirter, successfully used these scientific techniques to profit from the markets. However, over the ensuing decades, technology and financial theory have gradually pushed these scientific techniques to the side. Many traders and investors have now come to rely on academic financial theory and on the opinions of colorful media personalities appearing on television and the internet.

I have taken you on a wide ranging journey in this book and have sought to acquaint you with the mathematical and astrological links between investor emotion and market behavior. With this information, I sincerely hope you will now feel compelled to start applying this science to your trading and investing activity. I further hope you will share this information with others to ensure that the science does not come under threat of being lost or forgotten.

Meanwhile my personal quest to delve even deeper into the links between emotion and market behavior continues in earnest.

I will leave you with the following quote to accompany you on your journey of looking at the financial markets in a very different way.

"Perseverance leads to enlightenment. And the truth is more beautiful than your wildest dreams".

Neil Turok—theoretical physicist,
author of *The Universe Within*

ENDNOTES

Chapter 1

1. J.F. Scott, *History of Mathematics*, Taylor & Francis Publishers, London, 1969, pp58-64
2. W.W. Rouse Ball, *A Short Account of the History of Mathematics*, Dover Publications, New York, 1960, p. 167
3. S. Olsen, A. Stakhov, *The Mathematics of Harmony*, World Scientific Publishing, Singapore, 2009, pp 6-34
4. C. Carolan, *The Spiral Calendar*, New Classics Library, USA, 1992, pp28-27.
5. Oracle Thinkquest Foundation, http://library.thinkquest. org/27890/goldenRatio2p.html

Chapter 2

1. J. Long, *The Universal Clock*, P.A.S. Publishing, USA,

Chapter 3

1. D. Ferrera, *Gann for the Active Trader*, Traders Press Inc. 2006 USA, pp120-125

Chapter 4

1. H.S. Williams, *The Historians History of the World*, The Outlook Company, USA, 1904, pp 574-5

Chapter 5

1. R. Beck, *The Gartley Trading Method*, John Wiley & Sons, 2010, USA
2. H.M. Gartley, *Profits in the Stock Market*, 1935,
3. L. Pesavento, *Fibonacci Ratios with Pattern Recognition*, Traders Press, 1997, USA

Chapter 6

1. G. Stathis, *Business Astrology 101*, Starcycles Publishing, USA, 2001, pp129-147

Chapter 7

1. Moore, Douglas, A*strology, the Divine Science, Arcane Trust Publishing, USA, 1978, p189-90*
2. T.W. Griffon, *The Illustrated Guide to Astrology*, Bison Books Ltd, London, 1990, pp 100-110
3. G. Stathis, *Business Astrology 101*, Starcycles Publishing, USA, 2001, pp85-89
4. L. McWhirter, *McWhirter Theory of Stock Market Forecasting*, Astro Book Company, USA, 1938

Chapter 8

1. www.businesscycles.biz
2. www.stlouisfed.org
3. D. Ferrera, *Gann for the Active Trader*, Traders Press Inc. 2006 USA, pp. 124-125

Epilogue

1. N. Turok, *The Universe Within*, House of Anansi Press, Canada, 2012

GLOSSARY OF TERMS

Ascendant: One of four cardinal points on a horoscope, the Ascendant is situated in the East.

Aspect: The angular relationship between two planets measured in degrees.

Conjunct: An angular relationship of 0 degrees between two planets.

Descendant: One of four cardinal points on a horoscope, the Descendant is situated in the West.

Ephemeris: A daily tabular compilation of planetary and lunar positions.

Equinox: An event occurring twice annually, an equinox event marks the time when the tilt of the Earth's axis is neither toward or away from the Sun.

First Trade chart: A zodiac chart depicting the positions of the planets at the time a company's stock or a commodity future commenced trading on a recognized financial exchange.

First Trade date: The date a stock or commodity futures contract first began trading on a recognized exchange.

Full Moon: From a vantage point situated on Earth, when the Moon is seen to be 180 degrees to the Sun.

Geocentric Astrology: That version of astrology in which the vantage point for determining planetary aspects is the Earth.

Golden Mean: the unique mathematical solution to the quadratic equation $y^2-y—1 = 0$.

Grand Trine: a unique pattern in which 3 planets are 120 degrees separated from each other.

Hard Rectangle: a unique pattern of 4 planets (A, B, C, D) in which A is 135 degrees from B which is 45 degrees from C which is 135 degrees from D which in turn is 45 degrees from A.

Heliocentric Astrology: That version of astrology in which the vantage point for determining planetary aspects is the Sun.

Lunar Eclipse: A lunar eclipse occurs when the Sun, Earth, and Moon are aligned exactly, or very closely so, with the Earth in the middle. The Earth blocks the Sun's rays from striking the Moon.

Lunar Month: see Synodic Month

Metonic Cycle: a period of very close to 19 years

Mid-Heaven: One of four cardinal points on a horoscope, the Mid-Heaven is situated in the South.

New Moon: From a vantage point situated on Earth, when the Moon is seen to be 0 degrees to the Sun.

North Node of Moon: The intersection points between the Moon's plane and Earth's ecliptic are termed the North and South nodes. Astrologers tend to focus on the North node and Ephemeris tables clearly list the zodiacal position of the North Node for each calendar day.

Opposition: An angular relationship of 180 degrees between two planets.

Orb: The amount of flexibility or tolerance given to an aspect.

Phi: see the Golden Mean

Retrograde motion: The apparent backwards motion of a planet through the zodiac signs when viewed from a vantage point on Earth.

Rosetta: a unique pattern of 4 planets (A, B, C, D) in which A is 60 degrees from B which is 90 degrees from C which is 120 degrees from D which in turn is 90 degrees from A.

Sidereal Month: The Moon orbits Earth with a slightly elliptical pattern in approximately 27.3 days, relative to a fixed frame of reference (the Sun).

Sidereal Orbital Period: The time required for a planet to make one full orbit of the Sun as viewed from a fixed vantage point on the Sun.

Solar Eclipse: A solar eclipse occurs when the Moon passes between the Sun and Earth and fully or partially blocks the Sun.

Solstice: An event occurring twice annually, a solstice event marks the time when the Sun reaches its highest or lowest altitude above the horizon at noon.

Square: An angular relationship of 90 degrees between two planets.

Square of Nine: an array of numbers with starting point of 1. By moving clockwise and adding 1 unit, a square array can be constructed in which numbers in the array are related to one another by square root mathematics.

Synodic Month: During one sidereal month, Earth has also revolved part way around the Sun, making the average apparent time between one New Moon and the next New Moon longer than the sidereal month at approximately 29.5 days. Also called a lunar month.

Synodic Orbital Period: The time required for a planet to make one full orbit of the Sun as viewed from a fixed vantage point on Earth.

T-Square: a unique pattern of 3 planets (A, B, C) in which A is 180 degrees from B which is 90 degrees from C which is 90 degrees from A.

Thor's Hammer: a unique pattern of 3 planets (A, B, C) in which A is 135 degrees from B which is 135 degrees from C which is 90 degrees from A.

Transit Lines: a technique in which the longitudinal position of a planet is converted to price using the Universal Clock. The price reading is then plotted on a price chart of a stock or commodity.

Trine: An angular relationship of 120 degrees between two planets.

Universal Clock: the patented version of the Wheel of 24

Wheel of 24: a wheel divided into 24 segments of 15 degrees each. The inner potion of the Wheel contains degree readings 1 through 360. The outer portion of the Wheel contains price data. The Wheel allows for easy conversion of planetary longitudinal position to price.

Zodiac: an imaginary encircling the 360 degrees of the planetary system divided into twelve equal portions of 30 degrees each.

APPENDIX A

New Moon, Full Moon and Eclipse Data for 2013 and 2014

2013 Date	New Moon	Full Moon	2014 Date	New Moon	Full Moon
January 11	X		January 1	X	
January 27		X	January 16		X
February 10	X		January 30	X	
February 25		X	February 14		X
March 11	X		March 1	X	
March 27		X	March 16		X
April 10	X		March 30	X	
April 25 (L)		X	April 15 (L)		X
May 10 (S)	X		April 29 (S)	X	
May 25 (L)		X	May 14		X
June 8	X		May 28	X	
June 23		X	June 13		X
July 8	X		June 27	X	
July 22		X	July 12		X
August 6	X		July 26	X	
August 21		X	August 10		X
September 5	X		August 25	X	
September 19		X	September 9		X
October 5	X		September 24	X	
October 18 (L)		X	October 8 (L)		X
November 3 (S)	X		October 23 (S)	X	
November 17		X	November 6		X
December 3	X		November 22	X	
December 17		X	December 6		X
			December 22	X	

(S) Solar eclipse (L) Lunar eclipse

APPENDIX B

Using the Ephemeris

Appendix B

The 360 degrees zodiac is made up of 12 signs and each sign occupies 30 degrees. The starting point for a journey around the zodiac is 0 degrees of Aries. Figure B-1 presents a summary of the symbols used in astrology to denote the various planets and the various aspects. As you repeatedly apply the information in this book to your market activity, before long you will become quite fluent with these odd looking symbols.

Points		Zodiac Signs		Aspects	
☉	Sun	♈ Aries		☌	0° Conjunction
☾	Moon	♉ Taurus			Occultation, Tight ☌
☿	Mercury	♊ Gemini			Cazimi, ☉ eclipse
♀	Venus	♋ Cancer		⚺	30° Semi-sextile
⊕	Earth	♌ Leo		∠	45° Semi-square
♂	Mars	♍ Virgo		⚹	60° Sextile
⚳	Ceres	♎ Libra		□	90° Square
♃	Jupiter	♏ Scorpio		△	120° Trine
♄	Saturn	♐ Sagittarius		⚼	135° Sesquisquare
⚷	Chiron	♑ Capricorn		⚻	150° Quincunx
♅	Uranus	♒ Aquarius		☍	180° Opposition
♆	Neptune	♓ Pisces			
♇ ⯓	Pluto				
☊	North Node				

Figure B-1

Figure B-2 presents an excerpt taken from an Ephemeris for the month of December 1980. Along the top of the data table are the symbols denoting the various planets. Along the left axis, the days of the month appear. In each column there appears a number expressed in degrees along with another strange looking symbol. Thus, for any given day in the month of December 1980, one can find the position of the Sun, the Moon and the various planets in terms of degrees and astrological sign. For example, on December 1, 1980 we can see that Saturn was 7 degrees 45 minutes in the sign of Libra and Jupiter was 6 degrees, 2 minutes in the sign of Libra. Mars was 6 degrees 45 minutes in Capricorn. With a little practice you will quite soon find yourself comfortably interpreting the data in an Ephemeris.

DECEMBER 1980 — **00:00 UT**

Day	Sid.t	☉	☽	☿	♀	♂	♃	♄	♅	♆	♇	☊	☊	⚸	⚷
M 1	4 40 1	8♐57'07	26♍25	22♏47	8♏34	6♑47	6♎ 2	7♎45	26♏40	21♐54	23♎26	13°R24	14♌ 9	26♎45	14°R43
T 2	4 43 57	9°57'58	8♎17	24°16	9°48	7°33	6°11	7°49	26°43	21°56	23°27	13♌20	14° 6	26°51	14♉40
W 3	4 47 54	10°58'50	20° 7	25°45	11° 2	8°19	6°19	7°54	26°47	21°58	23°29	13°13	14° 3	26°58	14°37
T 4	4 51 50	11°59'43	1♏59	27°15	12°16	9° 5	6°28	7°59	26°51	22° 0	23°31	13° 4	14° 0	27° 5	14°35
F 5	4 55 47	13° 0'37	13°55	28°45	13°31	9°51	6°36	8° 3	26°54	22° 2	23°33	12°53	13°57	27°12	14°32
S 6	4 59 43	14° 1'33	25°58	0♐16	14°45	10°37	6°44	8° 7	26°58	22° 5	23°34	12°42	13°53	27°18	14°30
S 7	5 3 40	15° 2'29	8♐10	1°47	16° 0	11°24	6°53	8°12	27° 1	22° 7	23°36	12°30	13°50	27°25	14°27
M 8	5 7 36	16° 3'27	20°31	3°19	17°14	12°10	7° 1	8°16	27° 5	22° 9	23°38	12°19	13°47	27°32	14°25
T 9	5 11 33	17° 4'26	3♑ 3	4°51	18°29	12°56	7° 8	8°20	27° 8	22°11	23°39	12°11	13°44	27°38	14°22
W10	5 15 30	18° 5'25	15°44	6°23	19°43	13°42	7°16	8°24	27°12	22°14	23°41	12° 5	13°41	27°45	14°20
T 11	5 19 26	19° 6'25	28°36	7°55	20°58	14°29	7°24	8°28	27°16	22°16	23°43	12° 2	13°38	27°52	14°17
F 12	5 23 23	20° 7'26	11♒39	9°27	22°12	15°15	7°31	8°32	27°19	22°18	23°44	12°D 1	13°34	27°59	14°15
S 13	5 27 19	21° 8'28	24°56	11° 0	23°27	16° 1	7°39	8°36	27°23	22°21	23°46	12° 1	13°31	28° 5	14°13
S 14	5 31 16	22° 9'30	8♓27	12°32	24°41	16°48	7°46	8°40	27°26	22°23	23°47	12° 2	13°28	28°12	14°11
M15	5 35 12	23°10'32	22°13	14° 5	25°56	17°34	7°53	8°43	27°30	22°25	23°49	12°R 3	13°25	28°19	14° 8
T 16	5 39 9	24°11'35	6♈16	15°38	27°11	18°21	8° 0	8°47	27°33	22°27	23°50	12° 2	13°22	28°25	14° 6
W17	5 43 5	25°12'38	20°34	17°11	28°26	19° 7	8° 7	8°50	27°36	22°30	23°52	12° 0	13°18	28°32	14° 4
T 18	5 47 2	26°13'41	5♉ 6	18°44	29°40	19°54	8°13	8°54	27°40	22°32	23°53	11°55	13°15	28°39	14° 2
F 19	5 50 59	27°14'45	19°47	20°17	0♐55	20°41	8°20	8°57	27°43	22°34	23°54	11°49	13°12	28°46	14° 0
S 20	5 54 55	28°15'49	4♊30	21°51	2°10	21°27	8°26	9° 0	27°47	22°36	23°56	11°42	13° 9	28°52	13°58
S 21	5 58 52	29°16'54	19° 8	23°25	3°25	22°14	8°32	9° 3	27°50	22°39	23°57	11°35	13° 6	28°59	13°56
M22	6 2 48	0♑17'59	3♋33	24°58	4°39	23° 1	8°39	9° 6	27°53	22°41	23°58	11°29	13° 3	29° 6	13°54
T 23	6 6 45	1°19'05	17°39	26°32	5°54	23°48	8°44	9° 9	27°56	22°43	23°59	11°24	12°59	29°13	13°52
W24	6 10 41	2°20'11	1♌23	28° 7	7° 9	24°34	8°50	9°12	28° 0	22°45	24° 1	11°22	12°56	29°19	13°51
T 25	6 14 38	3°21'17	14°41	29°41	8°24	25°21	8°56	9°14	28° 3	22°48	24° 2	11°D22	12°53	29°26	13°49
F 26	6 18 34	4°22'24	27°36	1♑16	9°39	26° 8	9° 1	9°17	28° 6	22°50	24° 3	11°23	12°50	29°33	13°47
S 27	6 22 31	5°23'32	10♍ 9	2°51	10°54	26°55	9° 6	9°19	28° 9	22°52	24° 4	11°24	12°47	29°39	13°46
S 28	6 26 28	6°24'40	22°25	4°26	12° 9	27°42	9°12	9°22	28°12	22°54	24° 5	11°26	12°44	29°46	13°44
M29	6 30 24	7°25'48	4♎27	6° 1	13°23	28°29	9°17	9°24	28°16	22°57	24° 6	11°R27	12°40	29°53	13°43
T 30	6 34 21	8°26'57	16°22	7°37	14°38	29°16	9°21	9°26	28°19	22°59	24° 7	11°27	12°37	0♏ 0	13°41
W31	6 38 17	9♑28'07	28♎13	9♑13	15♐53	0♒ 3	9♎26	9♎28	28♏22	23♐ 1	24♎ 8	11♌25	12♌34	0♏ 6	13♉40

Delta T = 51.31 sec.

created from Swiss Ephemeris, Copyright Astrodienst AG [26.8.2012]

Figure B-2

So, for example, if you were trying to project forward from a significant high or low on the market to that time when Saturn had advanced, say, 30 degrees you would identify the day of the significant high or low, find that day in your Ephemeris, determine the degree position of Saturn and then look forward in the Ephemeris until you find the day when Saturn had advanced 30 degrees.

The one market cycle that is a bit testy to work with is that of Mars-Saturn. If trying to project forward by one Mars-Saturn cycle from a significant high or low, find that day in the Ephemeris and make a note of the position of Mars and also of Saturn. Make a note of the number of degrees that separate them—this is critical to your calculations. Mars is a faster moving planet than Saturn. Next, you will want to look forward in the Ephemeris until you find that date when Mars has made one complete 360 degree trip around the zodiac. As Mars has been moving through the zodiac, Saturn has also been moving—just a lot slower. With the position of Mars pinpointed, look slightly forward in the Ephemeris and maybe slightly backwards too. What you are looking for is that time when Mars and Saturn are at separated by the same number of degrees as they were at the outset. With a little practice, a person can quickly become adept at navigating through the Ephemeris.

INDEX

ABOUT THE AUTHOR

Malcolm Bucholtz, B.Sc, MBA is a graduate of Queen's University Faculty of Engineering in Canada and Heriot Watt University in Scotland where he received an MBA degree. He resides in western Canada where he trades the financial markets using technical chart analysis, esoteric mathematics and the astrological principles outlined in this book. He maintains both a website (www.investingsuccess.ca) and a blog (www.astrologicaltrading.wordpress.com) where he provides traders and investors with astrological insights into the financial markets.